I did not enjoy reading this book. Mostly, it pushed my emotional and theological buttons to such a degree that I was forced to think about things I don't want to face. Which is why I needed this book. You may not like what's within—but you *need* what is within. More than anything, Mikalatos and Khang disrupt just about every one of our false notions of tranquility by inviting us into the tender difficulties of the extravagant kindness of God.

> **A. J. SWOBODA, PhD**, associate professor of Bible, theology, and world Christianity at Bushnell University and author of *After Doubt*

The beauty and brilliance of *Loving Disagreement* is not just the wisdom and thoughtfulness of its content but also the way in which Kathy Khang and Matt Mikalatos model how to have kind, God-honoring discourse that deepens their understanding and respect for one another. In a church and world in which divisiveness and defensiveness are the norm, *Loving Disagreement* provides welcome reassurance that it is possible this side of heaven to experience unity without sacrificing or abandoning our unique opinions, heritages, and convictions. I'm so grateful to Kathy and Matt for having created this gracious, honest, and unique resource, because this is a book we need now more than ever.

> **HELEN LEE**, speaker and coauthor of *The Race-Wise Family*

I've spent the last few years wondering what it actually looks like for "us" (in the grand sense of the word) to live together. A lot of that wondering comes from a place of sadness and disillusionment, namely because of my experiences of online interactions. I find myself sincerely hopeful after reading *Loving Disagreement*. Matt and Kathy write from a place of sincere interest and lived experience. They actually like people.

I love the way the book is creatively structured, and I love the clarity with which they present pieces of lived wisdom *as well as* questions and concerns they're still working with. In short, I finished this book feeling not only less alone but also reenergized to help build and make room for loving community.

JUSTIN McROBERTS, author of *Sacred Strides*

Some people love disagreement and seek it with vengeance. Others hate it and do everything they can to avoid it. Matt and Kathy, in this book, offer a third way. They challenge the status quo as living examples of people who disagree in a loving way, a posture that finds its roots in the teachings of Jesus. Their back-and-forth conversation helps us see how much our culture, gender, upbringing, and life experiences influence our perceptions. This book is a life study that applies the sacred teachings of Jesus to our humanity through a practical spirituality that can lead us to a genuine unity.

TERRY M. WILDMAN, lead translator and project manager of
First Nations Version: An Indigenous Translation of the New Testament

Reading *Loving Disagreement* felt like sitting around a dinner table, over a warm meal, with good friends. Kathy and Matt show us what it looks like to honor and learn from each other. Personal stories are beautifully woven into each chapter, and I was profoundly moved as I read the humility in the back-and-forth responses between the authors. Thank you for the reminder that cultivating the fruit of the Spirit in our own lives and communities is a worthy cause.

JOHNNA HARRIS, cohost of *The Bodies Behind the Bus* podcast

In *Loving Disagreement*, we join Kathy and Matt for a vulnerable, brave, and timely conversation that meets our complex cultural moment. They will challenge us to bypass the brittle tools of toxic people-engagement into a subtle, surprising invitation through the fruit of the Spirit: a more faithful *metric* for engaging conflict. Through personal stories filled with wit and grace, Kathy and Matt share hard truths in ways that feel winsome and prophetic. Their conversations explore relational themes ranging from the importance of language; to toxic Christian culture; to race, gender, and ableism. Yet in the end we are left with hope in God's multifaceted love that can weave people together . . . even make them friends. I encourage everyone to pick up several copies of this book, hand them to your friends (and frenemies), and let the conversations begin.

JOSÉ HUMPHREYS III, author of *Seeing Jesus in East Harlem* and coauthor of *Ecosystems of Jubilee*

Why does meaningful connection to other people feel like a vanishingly rare experience? Maybe it's the very fact that we're more connected than ever that has revealed we have deep, significant differences that can't be chalked up to agreeing to disagree. How do we build relational bridges across such real gulfs? Khang and Mikalatos use the fruit of the Spirit to dive beyond clichés and into the real work of relationships. Their wisdom is not easily applied, but for those who want to experience the kind of oneness Jesus promises to his followers, the picture they paint is inviting and full of hope.

JR. FORASTEROS, author of *Empathy for the Devil*

Khang and Mikalatos stir the imagination for a different way to engage with differences and conflict. Funny, candid, and refreshingly frank, this book is helpful because it unveils the postures we accidentally assume are Christian and replaces them with the fruit of the Spirit. The book's dynamic format allows us to listen in (and learn tons) as two insightful and witty folks who really have an eye on society converse. It's like getting to sit at the table in a restaurant that is having the most fun. Khang and Mikalatos reveal their own disagreements in modeling a new way forward that gives me hope for the future of Christian presence in the public sphere. Thank you!

NIKKI TOYAMA-SZETO, executive director of Christians for Social Action

This book is a tool and resource for those trying to understand the art and gifts of bridge building and courageous conversations. The many things that divide us will eventually burn, and what will be left? Khang and Mikalatos do an excellent job of showing us that what truly matters is our collective connection to one another because of our citizenship within the Kingdom of God. Imagine if discourse began with this truth, with the reality of our connected humanity.

LATASHA MORRISON, author of *New York Times* bestseller *Be the Bridge: Pursuing God's Heart for Racial Reconciliation*

KATHY KHANG &
MATT MIKALATOS

Loving
Disagreement

FIGHTING FOR COMMUNITY
THROUGH THE FRUIT OF THE SPIRIT

NavPress

A NavPress resource published in alliance
with Tyndale House Publishers

Kathy: *To Peter, Bethany, Corban, and Elias for loving me and one another. And to all the haters: God loves us all.*

Matt: *To everyone who ever disagreed with me or loved me, and especially the people who did both.*

Contents

Introduction

Good Intentions Aren't Enough

Matt

A while back, my dear friend and editor Caitlyn reached out to me with a question, one that emerged from the angst and human discord we see and know all too well: "Could you write a book about how to get along when we disagree?"

She and her team had been talking about civility in the church. How should Christians interact with one another when they have disagreements? How should followers of Jesus interact in an increasingly polarized political climate?

She said I was someone who came to mind as trustworthy to write about all that because she's seen me strive to host kind, nuanced discussions about difficult topics on my social media. It's something I have a particular passion for, whether we're talking about abortion, theological differences, LGBTQ+ issues, or politics. My social-media community has grown to (mostly) respect each other even when they seriously disagree.

I'd been asked to write that kind of book before, but I had always turned those requests down. I wasn't convinced I had enough insight.

But Caitlyn and the wise folks at NavPress had another idea too: What if the book had two authors? What if the coauthors had different experiences, approaches, and ideas? What if they even disagreed sometimes?

Then Caitlyn floated the name of a person I love and respect a great deal: Kathy Khang.

Kathy is an activist, a voice for change, a person who speaks her mind and is ferociously protective of the vulnerable. She's the author of the amazing book *Raise Your Voice*,[1] among other things, and despite our mutual affection for each other we're vastly different people. I'm a white man born in the United States, while Kathy is a woman of color, an immigrant, and a naturalized citizen of the US. She lives near Chicago; I'm on the west coast.[2] I'm inclined to explore different possibilities in a conversation or issue to the point of uncertainty, and Kathy's quick-minded clarity cuts through the uncertainty with assurance and direction.

We have a lot in common, too: We both love Jesus; we have some similar concerns about Christian communities today; we've both been full-time missionaries in the past; we both have families; we both love to write; and despite our really different approaches, we both deeply care about people. All of which to say: I immediately knew both that Caitlyn had chosen the perfect cowriter and that Kathy would never agree to do it.

Although Caitlyn had pitched a compelling idea and an amazing coauthor, I decided not to mention it to Kathy. I planned to politely decline on behalf of us both. But then our mutual friend JR. asked me a wise question: "Why are you saying no for Kathy?"

Kathy

This book almost didn't happen because I almost didn't know about it. Matt was going to say no before asking his potential coauthor. When Matt and I talked about why he'd at first decided not to ask me, it dawned on me that we had stumbled into part of the issue we are trying to address in this book. We are well-meaning. We have good intentions. We think we know each other, what each other's motivations are, and ultimately what we would do in each other's situation.

But we don't.

Thankfully Matt talked with J.R., who talked some sense into Matt. Matt asked me, and, although we are friends, my answer was not what he expected. And when we talked about how this all came about, Matt was a little embarrassed that he thought he could speak on my behalf. I told him that as a woman of color and a former campus minister, I was completely used to it. Christian "brothers" have always thought it was their job to protect me, speak for me, and correct me.

Sure, I had been telling him and our podcast cohosts/friends that I wasn't sure if I would continue writing in the Christian space, whether I had anything else to say, or if I had the energy. But what Matt didn't know was that the invitation to tackle the public bickering and fighting together was the perfect project—because what I do have energy for is to build a few more bridges of understanding between people, between Christians.

Matt

As Kathy and I started talking, we quickly realized there was one more issue. That original word, *civility*, isn't something of particular use for Christians. Civility is about politeness. It's about courtesy within society and politics. Civility not only is an astonishingly low bar for Christians, who are called to much more than politeness, but it has also been used as a tool for the powerful to ignore the cries of the vulnerable. If a person in poverty, for instance, cries, "You're literally killing us with your ravenous greed!" we might respond, "Well, that's not the correct way to approach us about this issue." Civility says, *Your approach seems unpleasant, unkind, unfriendly. See if you can politely share your grievances.*

Civility can get in the way of helping those who need help. In the ER, for example, there's not always time for politeness. A doctor may not ask the name of a patient in respiratory distress before intubating them.

Sometimes, when polite requests for justice go unanswered, we have to move on to more aggressive requests (or demands). Kathy's experiences as a woman of color certainly give her deeper and better insights into this than I have. I'm far more likely to get what I need through civil discourse than she is. That's interesting and important and one of the reasons we wanted to write this book together: Disagreeing well as the people of God doesn't look just one way. Kathy's and my different approaches give just a glimpse into the complexity of what it means to live Spirit-formed lives in a fractured culture.

Kathy and I came back to the NavPress folks with a modified idea. What if, instead of talking about civility, we talked about something more difficult, more painful, and more honest? Followers of Jesus are called to something more impressive than simple politeness. We're called to things like love, patience, kindness, faithfulness. But how can we possibly be kind in the midst of these horrific disagreements? How can we move past anger and hatred and find patience and love?

That's what this book is about.

Most of us are tired of the incessant bickering and backbiting, even when it's focused on important issues. But Kathy and I believe there's a way to live out effective, productive, loving disagreement that moves us closer to Jesus and the Kingdom of God.

Kathy

A final and important note: As we go through this book, we will remind you that I am not white. I came to the United States when I was eight months old and became a US citizen more than thirty years later. English was originally my second language, even though now it is my primary language. White authors historically and still presently dominate the published author space, even though there have been recent blips of willingness to talk about race, ethnicity, culture, sexuality, and gender. Matt and I are both published authors, but the publishing world, while slowly changing, is *slowly* changing.

How we draw attention to this reality is going to emerge in this book in a few different ways. One is how we handle non-English words. I am in my fifties, and for my entire life I used the term *broken English* to describe my parents' English language skills. It wasn't until recently that the phrase began to irritate me. It's demeaning and dishonoring to my parents and all the other people whose primary language isn't English. A country that does not have an official language still operates under an assumption that there is a correct way to write and speak English. English is the default, the norm.

Traditionally in English-language books, non-English words are italicized, signaling to readers that this word or phrase is "not your normal." My coauthor is the one who brought this to our editorial team's attention, and we've decided to do away with that practice. Matt and I both live in the United States, but we are also part of the global church. No single language is the default, the norm.

This might seem like a small change, but it is part of the reason for this book and our approach. God did not create us to live and thrive independently. We are to be in community with people, and I am so thankful to be in community with Matt, my chingoo, my friend.

I wanted to write this book with Matt because this will be an opportunity to reach new readers who privately wonder why people like me make everything about race or gender when, in Christ, we are no longer Jew or Greek, slave or free, male or female.[3] This is also a chance to remind myself and My Dear Readers that Jesus always invites us to love one another—even when we disagree, even when another Christian questions our faith, even when we question another Christian's faith. So as I write into issues that may feel unfamiliar to you or uncomfortable for you, know that love is what drives me. White people are not my enemy. Systems of power and the principalities of this world that prioritize some groups of people above others—those are our common enemy. Racism, sexism, and homophobia hurt everyone, including the people who perpetuate those things. When we do not see each other as fully human, we misunderstand what it means to be fully human ourselves.

I wanted to write this book with Matt because in the kind of angry discourse we see online and in Christian circles, Matt should and could be my enemy. He is a white man with social power. The system that upholds the often-unconscious belief that being white is both superior and the norm—what we're going to refer to as white supremacy in this book—affords him access and privilege. (Check out the glossary for a longer explanation of this and other complex terms.) And if the mention of white supremacy makes you even the slightest bit uncomfortable, I'm asking you to keep reading. You started this book because you wanted a better way. That starts with being okay with that discomfort and being open to listening to an unfamiliar voice.

Growing up reciting the Lord's Prayer in two languages has always meant there were many voices in my life forming my faith and daring me to ask questions not only about what I believed in but in how I would express those beliefs day-to-day. That's what we are doing in this book—offering two voices from two vantage points. Matt and I have some common experiences and we both love Jesus and hold some similar beliefs, but we approach disagreements—both in our physical environments and on social media—differently. We have very different ways of looking at and experiencing the world. You'll see some of that as you read on, and we hope as you get to know both of us you'll experience the freedom and gift of learning about and from different approaches. Because in that middle space where our differences and similarities intersect, where loving disagreements often happen, faith moves between the spiritual and physical and into our daily interactions.

CHAPTER I

WAR! WHAT IS IT GOOD FOR?

Disrupting the Polarization of God's Kingdom

Matt

I'VE GOTTEN MY SHARE of hate mail over the years, and all of it was from fellow Christians. I'm not talking about pleasant disagreements or even harsh but well-intended critiques. I'm referring to emails and physical letters filled with name-calling, threats of violence, even veiled references to hurting my children. Kathy's had that and then some, including a heckler who shouted at her from the audience while she was teaching at a chapel.

The reasons for those hateful letters varied. Sometimes it was because of a (in my eyes) small disagreement with something in one of my books. Sometimes it was because of a difference in politics. Occasionally the writer didn't like a speaker I invited to a conference. And more than once, it was because of a misunderstanding—I hadn't said or done what they thought I had.

I was a missionary for about twenty years, and sometimes my hate mail came from fellow missionaries. When I resigned from our mission organization and moved into writing full-time, I received an anonymous greeting card that ended with a statement along the lines of "I'm glad you're leaving the organization, and I'll see you in heaven (maybe)."

Is Christian Culture Getting Worse?

I have a lot of friends in the church whom I disagree with about a lot of things: politics, theology, whether this or that movie is actually good. Our friendship makes those disagreements easier to set aside because we love each other. But as society continues to fracture, as our media monetizes polarization and normalizes it for the rest of us, it's fair to ask whether the church is being affected.

From my point of view, the answer is almost certainly yes. If you're uncertain whether that's true, say something "controversial" on your favorite social-media platform and watch the replies, the critiques, the angry folks with torches and pitchforks. I've seen pastors—who presumably know better—get in name-calling competitions with strangers online. I saw a woman with a Bible verse about love in her profile call someone names so vile that the moderators of the social-media platform had to step in.

We've also gotten to the point where disagreements on secondary[1] theological issues (which can range from really important things, like the role of women in ministry, to relatively unimportant things, like whether you believe the Rapture comes before, after, or during the Tribulation—or not at all) are being called "heresy."[2] Too often I see brothers and sisters in Christ suggesting that everything they believe is a "gospel issue," implying that disagreement with them is disagreement with Christ himself. And we're collectively wrestling with some difficult theological and ethical questions as a church, too, so it's only natural that we might have some disagreements as we're trying to figure those things out.

Politics aren't helping, especially in the United States. A few years back, I was speaking at a men's retreat, and during a Q and A one of the brothers was pushing hard to get me to take a public stance on a political issue. (I had thoughts on the issue, but this was a retreat about spiritual disciplines.) So I asked the group a question: "Which do you spend more time doing—getting spiritual nourishment or watching your favorite news and political commentary?" Nearly every person (including me) had to admit they spent more time with their political commentators than the combined time they spent reading the Scriptures, praying, participating in church activities, doing ministry, and so on. Is it any wonder that we might sometimes discover we're putting politics or nation building above our brothers and sisters? And when our news sources start conflating their politics with our religious points of view—as many of them do—is it any surprise we start to think that someone who's "wrong" politically is also wrong spiritually?

It's not like we've never disagreed within the church before. Sometimes we've done it well, and sometimes we've done it poorly. I love the example of the United Methodists. The simple version of their story is that various denominations in the Methodist tradition had fractured from one another over theological and ethical questions as diverse as whether a Christian should participate in enslaving people to whether a Christian could join a "secret society" like the Freemasons. Over the decades, different pieces of the fractured community discovered they could at least minister together, and eventually some of those pieces came back together—liberals and conservatives and neoorthodox—and formed the "United Methodist" denomination. It's a great example of how listening to Jesus and loving each other and staying in communication tends to help us find our way back to each other, even amid serious disagreements. (Of course, as I write this, the same denomination is in the midst of yet another messy schism. How long will it take us to find our way back to each other again?)

But really every denomination has experienced some version of this. When I was a kid growing up in a Baptist church, it split when the pastor had an affair and started his own spin-off church. And for a few years in college, I attended a denomination that started because of a disagreement over whether it was necessary to stand up when reading Scripture aloud.[3]

Is the church getting worse, or is this something we've faced our entire history as imperfect people seeking to follow Jesus together?

I honestly don't know the answer to this question. I can say that it feels worse sometimes to me. But then again, there are some really encouraging signs too. When I was growing up, lots of my Baptist teachers told me Catholic believers were not Christians. I haven't heard that in a long time—after all, large portions of the church have been learning to work together on things that matter to all of us, and part of what brought Catholics and conservative evangelicals together seems to be an agreement about abortion. On the other hand, this same topic, among other things, is causing breaks in communion among conservative and progressive believers today.

Disagreements, fighting, and hatred. These things seem common in the wider community of Christendom today. Politics, theology, even personal preference create seemingly insurmountable rifts. I've seen this referred to as "war in heaven," which is such a fascinating phrase to me. The biblical "war in heaven" was between the angels and the demons (and was won handily by the angels at God's command). When we use that phrase of human beings, we build a narrative where I'm presumably on the side of the angels and my opponents are demons, and we lose sight of how we're all made in the image of God. But still, it's hard not to see ourselves "at war" when we are working hard to destroy each other.

We're not doomed to be stuck here, though. There is, Kathy and I believe, a twofold path out of this destructive war, out of seeing our brothers and sisters as enemies and demons—and into a spacious place of loving each other even as we disagree.

The first part of the path is our citizenship. The Bible says we are citizens of heaven.[4] Not of the United States or Canada or South Korea or any earthly kingdom. Our first allegiance is to the Kingdom of God. For me and Kathy, this idea resonates as key to this complicated question of disagreement.

The next step on the path—one we're going to spend most of this book on—is what Paul describes about the reality of being citizens of the Kingdom, equipped and empowered and motivated by the Holy Spirit as we engage with (and, yes, disagree with) one another. As followers of Jesus are planted in the Holy Spirit, the Spirit grows and bears good things in our lives—and relationships and communities are changed.

Citizens of Heaven

I was traveling overseas when I got stopped at a border and was asked a lot of questions about how many passports I have. The border guard was questioning me to make sure that I hadn't traveled to another country they were at war with and hidden that fact by using a second passport. And while some people have "dual citizenship" and may be citizens of two countries (and thus have two passports to choose from), I only have citizenship in the US, and I only have one passport.

Passports bring with them the advantages, privileges, and expectations of citizenship. For instance, if I had sought Greek citizenship when I was younger (something I'm qualified to do because my grandfather was Greek), I would have been expected to serve for a time in the Greek military: It's mandatory for all male citizens. But also, as a citizen of an EU country, I could have traveled within the EU, gotten a job there, or gone to school without a visa.

Paul talks about how he is a "pure-blooded citizen of Israel" in

Philippians 3:5 (NLT). He goes on to say that while some people only think about "this life here on earth" (verse 19), Paul isn't able to do that, and he doesn't think other Christ followers can do that either. We are citizens of heaven. We have dual citizenship here on earth, but we also have responsibilities, obligations, and privileges connected to heaven.

Jesus also talked often about the Kingdom of heaven and how his followers were part of that Kingdom. Because that citizenship is eternal, our loyalties and values should be placed first and foremost there, not centered in the places of our earthly citizenship.

When I lived overseas, those of us with shared citizenship back in the US felt a special bond. We loved things about the culture we lived in, but when we were with fellow citizens from "back home," we instantly gravitated toward what we had in common, even if we didn't know each other. The local consulate would host parties on the big holidays that all US citizens were welcome to attend. If you ran into another US citizen in a restaurant there was a lot of "Where are you from?" and "Remember Doritos? I wish we could get those here." When you share a homeland, you also share some cultural values, preferences, thoughts, and ideas.

This is one of the reasons that what's come to be known as "Christian nationalism" is so antithetical to what Scripture describes. As citizens of heaven, we owe our first allegiance not to a flag—any flag—but to Christ. The Kingdom of God doesn't have borders. It exists in every nation in the world. Full allegiance to an earthly nation demands that I prioritize that nation's interests above those of people from other nations . . . including those who are citizens of heaven. If our faith requires us to embrace nationalism in the country we live in, then Christians in the Congo or Russia or China or Afghanistan would be nationalists in their respective nations, too, and thus potentially in conflict with Christians outside their national borders. And so our Kingdom citizenship, our Kingdom identity, would become fractured, little more than a series of political conflicts (sound familiar?) rather than spiritual unity. But we are citizens of heaven. When our earthly nation and our heavenly Kingdom are in conflict (which happens often), Christians should always choose God's Kingdom.

Scripture even goes a step further, saying that we're not only citizens but ambassadors of Christ.[5] Which means that we have been sent into whatever nation we're in today as representatives of our heavenly Kingdom. Just as people overseas could see that I am an American and recognize some American values in the way I interacted, the people in the world should see the values, ideals, and culture of heaven in my life here.

It boils down to this: I should be living my life in such a way that when someone asks, "What is heaven like?" they should have a decent idea by looking at me. My culture and habits and thoughts and ideas should be foreign to them, unfamiliar . . . because I'm a citizen of another place.

Raising the Bar

The wrinkle for all of us is that every human citizen of the heavenly Kingdom is a naturalized citizen. None of us are physically born into it. Citizenship is available for anyone, but those of us who choose it have to go through a process of becoming. Which means that there are things for us to learn. When Kathy became a US citizen, she had to memorize dates and history and know how the US government functions—all things I never had to do as a birthright citizen, since I was born in California.

While becoming a citizen of heaven doesn't require a knowledge test, we're all in the process of learning what it means to grow and change and be shaped into someone who can be not only a productive citizen but also an ambassador on Christ's behalf.

Which is why, in the end, "civility" is not the ultimate goal of a believer in an argument. That's not to say we should actively be trying to be uncivil, but there are times when representing the Kingdom may seem rude to the world around us because the way of the Kingdom confronts and presses on places in which the world would prefer to stay comfortable. James tells us that true religion is taking care of the marginalized—orphans and widows—and to keep ourselves from being polluted by the world we're in.[6] Speaking up for the marginalized and refusing to stay silent in the face of injustice disrupts the status quo. And while ambassadors work hard to say things in the least disruptive and upsetting way possible, ambassadors also have a mission that drives what they do and how they do it.

Learning our heavenly culture and working as an ambassador to those outside the Kingdom takes time—a lifetime, probably. But we're not left to just figure it out on our own. There's a Person in charge of our training and ongoing education: the Holy Spirit.

Paul talks about this embodiment of the Spirit's work at length in the book of Galatians. The people at the Galatian church were in the middle of a gigantic argument: As Christ-following non-Jews, were they responsible for following Jewish law? No way, Paul said. And he had strong words for those who said otherwise.

But he also talked about how, as the people in the church disagree, there's an easy way to tell if someone is following Christ. It's not by looking at the external obedience to the law but by looking to the singular rule that sets us free from the law: "Love your neighbor as yourself."[7]

He then warns that if we continually bite at each other, eventually we'll be consumed. So what's the answer? How can we live in a way that we won't destroy ourselves with our arguments? Paul says it's simple: "Live by the Spirit."[8]

When someone isn't living by the Spirit, that should be obvious because the sins in that person's life will be obvious. Paul lists some sins that we like to talk about a lot when judging others, like sexual immorality, drunkenness, worshiping something other than God. But he also lists a bunch of things our Christian community seems to have found ourselves helplessly accepting of—even some things we defend or try to say are good. Angry outbursts. Hostility and acts of hatred.

Dissension. Discord. Factions.[9] So many of these things are "just the way it is" in Christian culture today.

When we find that someone or something—a friend, a spiritual authority, a TV show, or an internet personality—constantly pushes us toward anger, encouraging us toward hatred or hostility or even fear, that's a warning sign. That's not how the Spirit works.

Paul tells us exactly what it looks like when someone has allowed the Spirit to transform their lives. He uses the metaphor of the Spirit bearing fruit in our lives. Once the Spirit is planted in us, we should expect there to be continual growth that leads to "love, joy, peace, patience, kindness, goodness, faithfulness, gentleness, and self-control."[10] That's far more difficult than mere civility.

So that's our path through the war we find ourselves in. How do we, in the midst of really important and meaningful disagreements, raise the bar on our expectations for how we treat one another and the people around us? How do we let the Spirit bear fruit in ways that are meaningful and real and matter for the people we know and the questions we confront?

At the end of every chapter, we're going to have a chat, friend to friend, human to human, about the ways we agree and disagree about what the other person wrote. We love each other, and we're not always on the same page—and we're better Jesus followers for leaning into these conversations.

Kathy

Matt, we agree that civility is too low a bar for Christians. I think the bar is too low for Christians who have thought of themselves as the majority in the North American context: white Christians who have historically held power and privilege, and men living in a world filled with systems created by men. In our time of global disruption, many people who are used to being at the center of power are being forced to consider a future that looks very different.

With a broad brush, I will also say people of color have been more than civil. Historically, Christians in the United States have perpetuated harm against minority groups—through genocide, forced relocation, slavery, and much more. They have frequently justified these actions by appealing to their fidelity to Jesus, failing to grapple with how these actions have reinforced the dominance of a white majority culture, a priority that does not come from Jesus. The Christianity that coalesces around these biases then admonishes people to find their identity first and only in Christ, diminishing and marginalizing the distinctiveness of their ethnicity, culture, or race, and implicitly setting the norms of a white majority culture at the center of Christian expression. Ironically, the white Christianity that emerges then tells people of color to be colorblind.

People of color have shown great patience. But, Matt, I know you and I are both hopeful that enough Christians will be willing to take a breath, to extend to people of color the same civility as they do white folks, and see a path forward.

The language of citizenship is one of belonging and of privilege and responsibility. But an open door at church on Sunday rarely means belonging. It's just unlocked. Open doors don't mean an invitation to enter, to be an equal part of the community. Even if people of color feel welcomed or brave enough to walk through the door, rarely are we actually invited to shape what happens inside.

In many ways, we are writing this book because we individually and collectively have assumed we know what it means to be Christians, to be citizens of the Kingdom of God. But because we grew up in the church or adjacent to Christian culture, we never really had to think about the ins and outs, nor were we ever questioned and challenged about our beliefs.

My husband and I are both Korean American, but he and my children are all American born. They have always been US citizens, so it is jarring still when *any* of us gets asked—not once but repeatedly—"Where are you from? No, where are you really from?"

I've heard a lot of talk about who is and isn't a Christian, and that actually still angers me because it sounds a lot like that language I hear from birthright citizens who consider themselves "true" Americans. I carried around a green card for decades (it wasn't actually green, folks), and that definitely shaped my understanding of belonging, citizenship, and civic duty and how Christians are supposed to engage in the world and culture around us. Matt, how do you think your status as a birthright citizen shaped your understanding of and comfort in the church?

Matt

Green cards aren't green? I've been lied to all these years!

Here's the reality of being a birthright citizen (especially one who is part of majority culture): I have never once stopped to think about it. I've taken it for granted. I'm always amazed, Kathy, by how seriously you take voting—how you volunteer at every election and work to make sure ballots are fair and accessible to legal voters. I grew up rolling my eyes at the privilege: "Ugh! Time to vote again!" Or at most I'd canvass for a political issue or candidate I was trying to convince others they should vote for—which is totally fine but really different from the kind of service you do, which is designed to be for the good of all citizens rather than "what I think is best" for others.

So yeah. I'd say that birthright citizenship *and* my "birthright Christianity" growing up evangelical were completely unexamined other than the occasional thought of *Wow, I'm lucky that I happened to be born in the greatest country in the world and also the one true faith*. True American and true believer, right?

Blind to my blessings and blind to my own assumptions, probably, is the answer.

Kathy

Well, my first green card was from the early seventies when I was a baby, and that card was green. Decades later, when I updated the card, the new ones weren't green. You also have to turn in the card when you are naturalized, and I still think about the group of people at my naturalization ceremony each turning in our green cards before swearing our allegiance to the United States of America.

Matt, you write about living overseas and being asked, "Where are you from?" by other US citizens. You all knew you were US citizens because you were invited by the consulate, so my heart died a little reading that knowing that you were being asked the question as a way of connection. I still get asked that question, and it hurts the most when it comes from non-Asian Christians—because it's not a way to find common ground but to point out a difference. Sometimes it's even a way of "othering" me. Sure, I'm a naturalized citizen, but I am from the Chicago suburbs. That rarely is the answer people are looking for, though. Please speak for all non-Asian Christians and tell me why that is so often a starting place for conversation.

Matt

Hmm. Okay, I think this answer is going to go a little differently than you think, Kathy, but I'm trying to be honest here from a non-Asian Christian point of view.

First of all, we can just acknowledge together that the core assumption many of us have when we say "American" is that we're talking about a white person. If I say, "Picture a legal immigrant coming to America for the first time" (go ahead, try it), most of us picture someone in the 1920s coming in past the Statue of Liberty, and almost none of us picture Angel Island or the slave trade or even modern immigration. (Refugees, for instance, are legal immigrants but probably not the first people we picture when we talk about legal immigration.) And it's not just white folks who do it! Kathy, you've told me before that you get the "where are you from" question from people of multiple ethnicities and races.

So, yes, part of the issue is that many of us look at someone with Asian features and the first thought is: *Where are they from?* We assume they're not "from America," even though, aside from Native Americans, most of us aren't "from America" in that sense. The second part is that this actually is an attempt at connection. It's wrongheaded, it's hurtful, and it reveals some unconscious internalized white supremacy, but none of that is intended. It's honestly an attempt to create common ground.

We can see evidence of this desire for common ground because if, for instance, you were to say "Korean," the person will go on to say something like "I love Korean food!" or "My cousin was adopted from Korea" or "Is it hard to write in Korean characters?" Now, again, these responses are all potentially problematic and hurtful, too, but I'm talking about intent here. The person has no idea this reveals prejudice. They have no idea this is "othering." They really, honestly, think they are being nice and kind and friendly . . . which is why it can be so upsetting to them (or I should probably say "us") when it's pointed out as hurtful.

The great irony here is that in most ethnic-minority communities, the connection to one's ethnic legacy, family, and family history is treasured and important, much more than in many majority-culture communities. So underneath the question is something that many Asian Americans would love to share, but the ask is so clumsy and hurtful that the possibility gets (rightfully) shut down.

On the flip side, these questions can be so painful because they are rooted in assumptions about what is the default or "normal." Even the terms *majority/minority*, which I'm using here, are complex: people of Asian heritage, not white people, are a majority in the world. And as various people are assimilated into whiteness as a cultural norm, being "white" robs people of ethnic identity (I'm Greek and Irish, not just "white"), just like the term "Asian American" flattens a broad diversity of ethnicities and cultures into a single ("nonwhite") category. In situations like these, differences of terminology, understanding levels, experience, or our relationship to one another can create discomfort, misunderstandings, or conflict.

Our struggle to connect with and honor diverse backgrounds is a great example of how we can come to these points of conflict where we're hurting each other without intending to hurt each other. And then we get entrenched in our different positions and can't find a way back to one another. We end on the one side with people saying, "Don't be so sensitive. I wasn't trying to hurt your feelings!" and on the other side, people saying, "You could try not actively harming me and others!"

Where I land in moments like this: If I'm not trying to harm someone, I apologize for it and then try not to do it again. I don't ask the person who was harmed to take the initiative to "forgive and move on" over and over.

Anyway, Scripture says that one day every "nation, tribe, people and language" is going to be united in Christ.[11] I'd like to think that when that happens, our citizenship in Christ will be primary, and our nations, tribes, and languages will be things to be celebrated.

Kathy

Look at us. White supremacy and intentions in the first chapter. YES! White supremacy hurts all of us, including white people who may have lost most or even all ties to their cultural and ethnic heritage, instead assimilating to a flattened culture that can fall under the term *whiteness*. I hope when we get interviewed about this book, someone will ask you about that loss and the impact you think it has on your understanding of your family and of God. As a child, I was often embarrassed by my parents' accent and "broken" English, but I also knew there was something about being connected culturally that was different from the experiences of so many of my friends.

It wouldn't be until later I would learn that difference was beautiful and gave me a more vivid understanding of that picture of every tribe, tongue, and nation. Even now when my parents and I are talking about me gook saram (Americans), we know we are talking about white people. We aren't even talking about my kids and my nieces and nephews or even my sister or husband, who were all American born.

All that to say, I am not that surprised by the direction you went. I do appreciate you bringing up intent and how you respond when you are the one causing the hurt. Too many times, the perpetrator of harm demands that their intent is what is most important. So long as you didn't intend to harm, everyone should move on. As a Korean American woman, I am admittedly tired of having to give people a pass just because something wasn't intended to be harmful. I'm still learning how to communicate to others that intent does not erase impact. Sometimes the most loving thing I can do is to call someone into conversation about the racist, sexist, ableist thing they've said.

I'm still learning that myself. I've been running a virtual yoga class for women of color for several years. It started shortly after the racial uprising in 2020 in response to the murder of George Floyd. I saw so many of my activist friends, women of color, hitting the streets, organizing, educating, and I was concerned about their health. I send an email monthly with a few random thoughts and a link to the class. But in one of those emails, one of my own places of ignorance and prejudice came into full view.

My comments were ableist and rooted in white supremacy, and I received an email response. I'll be honest: My first reaction was *That's not what I meant.* I had to listen to my own advice. I stopped. I identified where I thought I was being misrepresented and why that bothered me. I got over myself and looked for where my comments had hurt and harmed this person and perpetuated stereotypes about mental health. And then I wrote back with an apology and asked if and how our relationship needed repair. I don't actually know this person. We are only connected through these weekly virtual yoga classes. But I also realized that this is how divisions can be sown or repaired.

I could've approached this situation with the posture of fighting an enemy. When I first read the email, I got defensive, felt hurt and misunderstood. If I had stayed in those emotions and reacted, I can guarantee my intent would've been to retaliate without concern for the relationship. But when we learn to cultivate lives rooted in the fruit of the Spirit, we're empowered and invited to engage in loving disagreements with a more Christlike posture, and the outcomes have the chance of reflecting the Spirit's deeper work in ourselves and between communities.

CHAPTER 2

A LOVING GOD AND LOVING PIZZA

Killing Westernized Love for a Radical Shift

Kathy

I CAN LOVE DEEP-DISH PIZZA and love all three of my children, but in those two cases how I express my love is different. I can go weeks, sometimes months, without deep-dish pizza with a butter crust, but if I haven't heard from any one of my now-adult children within the last few days, I'll text or call just to connect or hear their voice on their outgoing voicemail message.

Love in the English language is an all-purpose word for something between "I really like ___" and "till death do us part," which means the word both has many meanings and means almost nothing.

My first language was Korean, so I have other words available to me in conversations with my parents: jowa when I describe liking the food someone has prepared for me; sarang for the overwhelming care and concern I have for my family and friends that compels me into action. The words are not interchangeable because the objects and responses are different. If you do not have the benefit of speaking another language, your understanding and use of the single word in English is limiting, especially when it comes to articulating, understanding, and expressing the love God has for us and invites Christians to live.

Thankfully, the Bible was not originally written in English. Depending on which English version of the Bible you use, you are reading a translation or paraphrase of the original text, which was primarily written in Hebrew and Greek. It's important for us to remember this because communication and understanding involve context and tone often lost in interpretation. And the original authors of the Bible had multiple words available to them to describe not only the emotion but also the relationships and actions involved in each type of love.

Which Love Is Best?

In the Old Testament, there is only one Hebrew word for love—*'āhab* אהב; noun: 'ahăḇâ—and it covers the same broad ground as the English word. But when we get to the New Testament and the Greek words for love, things get beautifully complicated and interesting with opportunities for misunderstanding. Sounds like love, doesn't it?

In the Greek world of the New Testament, there were several words used for love—and four that matter when it comes to loving disagreement[1]:

- *storge* (στοργή): a familial affection or devotion[2]
- *philia* (φιλία): a love between siblings or friends, based on experience and an overarching compassion and mutual respect[3]
- *eros* (ἔρως): erotic love[4]
- *agapē* (ἀγάπη): love or goodwill[5]

The Greek word *storge* is not found in the Bible. Its opposite—*astorgos* (ἄστοργος)—is used in Romans 1:31 and 2 Timothy 3:3 to describe someone as "unloving"; "without natural affection"; "hard-hearted towards kindred."[6] *Philostorgos* (φιλόστοργοι), a compound word from *philos* and *storge* meaning fond of natural relatives, is only found once in Scripture: in Romans 12:10, which commands believers to be devoted to one another with familial affection.[7]

The next Greek word that has been translated into English as *love* is *philia* (φιλία), commonly referred to as "friendship love." You may recognize it as the root for *Philadelphia*, the city of brotherly love. This word is found often in secular Greek texts and throughout the Bible, including in John 11:3, when Martha and Mary let Jesus know that Lazarus "the one whom you love [*phileō*, verb form of the adjective *philia*] is ill" (CEB), and in Matthew 10:37 when Jesus tells the disciples they cannot be worthy of Jesus if they love (*phileō*) their parents more than they love (*phileō*) Jesus.

Eros (ἔρως) is another Greek word for love that's not in the Bible. *Eros* is the sensual, erotic, sexual-attraction kind of love. We see mostly negative expressions of this idea throughout the Bible, with the notable exception of the book of Song of Songs. The relationship between Jesus and the church, the Bride of Christ, is often explained through marriage, and yet we must remember that our understanding of marriage is tainted and impacted by a Hollywood/Hallmark expression of love and sexual and romantic attraction. Biblical marriage wasn't about Insta-worthy proposals and weddings. Culturally it was commercial and transactional. Only when you read Song of Songs as an allegory of love between lovers can you imagine a different kind of love between spouses and then perhaps between Jesus and the church: a relationship based on mutuality, love focused on the pleasure and flourishing of the other and not on power and shame.

Finally, we get to *agape* (ἀγάπη), which is simply translated as *love* or *goodwill*. I don't know about you, but I remember more than one sermon explaining that *agape* is the best or highest of the "loves": God's unconditional, sacrificial, pure, and perfect love for humankind. In fact, the ranking of loves often focuses on a conversation between Jesus and Peter.

> When they had finished eating, Jesus said to Simon Peter, "Simon son of John, do you love [*agapas*] me more than these?"
>
> "Yes, Lord," he said, "you know that I love [*philō*] you."
>
> Jesus said, "Feed my lambs."
>
> Again Jesus said, "Simon son of John, do you love [*agapas*] me?"
>
> He answered, "Yes, Lord, you know that I love [*philō*] you."
>
> Jesus said, "Take care of my sheep."
>
> The third time he said to him, "Simon son of John, do you love [*philō*] me?"
>
> Peter was hurt because Jesus asked him the third time, "Do you love [*philō*] me?" He said, "Lord, you know all things; you know that I love [*philō*] you."
>
> Jesus said, "Feed my sheep."[8]

People have spent a lot of ink and airtime on this exchange because of Jesus' repetition, asking Peter the same question three times. In English, the passage is translated as "love"—Jesus asking Peter over and over, "Do you love me?" and Peter answering over and over, "Yes, I love you." In Greek, the alternate usage of *agapas* and *philō* has some sort of ranking or elevation of one type of love over another, but Jesus' initial use of *agapas* isn't meant to impose a heavier burden or expectation on Peter, nor is Jesus' use of *philō*, the word Peter uses in his responses, a lowering of the type of love Jesus is referring to.

Perhaps Jesus isn't presenting a hierarchy of love. Perhaps he's instead walking Peter through the last time Peter was asked about his relationship to Jesus, when Peter denied knowing Jesus three times in Jesus' final hours. And perhaps the misunderstanding and clarification between Jesus and Peter is also an example of how disagreements start but do not have to end in more division.

If we take this conversation within the context of the whole of their relationship, this may not be a lessening of expectations from a perfect love to a friendship love but rather an invitation for Peter to once again be friends with Jesus, to care about the things and people Jesus cares about. (Also, can someone explain to me why it changes from *lambs* to *sheep*? That seems like a bigger question!)

The elevation of *agapē* as the "highest" and perfect love expressed not only by God but by Jesus' followers is a socially located concept. It's only within the Christian tradition that the two words are ranked. Some theologians and pastor types have argued that because *agapē* is used more in the New Testament than *phileō*, it is the "better" or more perfect love. From a cultural-context standpoint, that simply wasn't the case: The word *agapē* was not used as often as *phileō* in secular Greek writing. Just because it appears more often in the Bible doesn't mean it's "holier" and more important. And we should also be on guard against the very Western value of "more is better."

Going back to the conversation between Jesus and Peter, perhaps what we should focus on is that both words for love are used. Both are important to how Jesus and Peter relate to each other and how Peter will love those entrusted to him. All the facets of love are vital as we interrogate whether we're just assenting to a theoretical sort of love—or truly operating out of the Spirit in action.

Love Is . . .

As a writer, I am a fan of words—their meanings, roots, connotations. When broken down to its Greek roots, *philanthropy* means "love of humanity." *Agapē* can also be translated as *charity*.

When you think of charity, what comes to mind?

The Christian church in the United States is classified as a charitable organization, which means it cannot be taxed. That is why those who donate to churches and religious organizations can claim that gift as tax-deductible. When you give to charity, how does that factor into your decision making? Do you only give to organizations that offer a tax deduction?

Churches and other faith-based organizations do and have done great work in providing different services for communities. During the COVID-19 pandemic, a Catholic church in my community permanently expanded its food pantry to better serve the ever-increasing number of individuals and families needing help. The pantry is set up like a grocery store where people can shop for their own groceries with a degree of dignity and autonomy. I live in a suburb; the assumption had been that there wasn't much of a need for assistance in our community, and yet reality has proven that is not the case.

But what also popped up were shelves inside the local high schools, places where people could leave nonperishables for students to grab, even when school was not in person, and some residents turned their Little Free Library into a place where neighbors could pick up a book and a box of pasta. Charity and love for one another was not limited to the church or a tax receipt.

Maybe when you think of charity, you reflect on that short-term mission trip; or the kids who participated in soccer camp after sitting through a short Bible story; or the bags of clothes you no longer want, need, or can wear. What are the long- and short-term impacts of your actions of charity, and are your actions loving? Would you give your family bags of used clothes you no longer want and consider that loving? Would you accept that same bag of used clothes as a loving act from your family or friends or even God? Sometimes what we think of as charity and loving our neighbors is just an act of convenience—for ourselves—or even a show of support for our political or theological beliefs.

Years ago, when my children were younger, I made it a practice to save all the shoeboxes from shoes we had purchased that year. We would spend a few days after Thanksgiving buying highly breakable trinkets, pencils, and other cheap items to fill those shoeboxes to be shipped to poor children in other countries. It made me feel good about myself and my intentions, and it was a visual lesson for my family: *Look at how many shoes we bought for your growing feet, and look at how many little kids are going to appreciate those boxes filled with stuff.* And then some loving Christian friends who saw what I couldn't see pointed out that just because children are poor doesn't mean they should receive junk. Also, just because they are poor doesn't mean they celebrate Christmas. Insert face-palm.

Christians should be known for our love, so the next time you do something charitable, think about being on the receiving end of that action. Would you receive that as loving and reflective of God's love for us?

When we think about love in our disagreements, we probably tend to think more in terms of restraint: *I'm loving that person by not saying what I really think. I'm loving that person by being nicer to them than they deserve.* But for Christians, love is an action, which means we have to really think about what we're doing to move *toward* people in love—even, and maybe even especially, the ones we disagree with. A word of caution and freedom for My Dear Readers: Moving toward people we disagree with in love does not mean putting ourselves in the way of harm. This is particularly true for people of color and disabled and LGBTQ+ people. Love in action can be drawing healthy boundaries or inviting the other person to do some learning before re-engaging in conversation.

What does this look like practically? One way is to think about which causes or organizations you support financially or even which businesses you support or have chosen to boycott. When you act in charity, is your first impulse to be loving? Who are the people who disagree with your choices, and how do you engage in those disagreements with love? Let's make sure we're actually putting *agapē* and *philō* into action and identify the places where our motives—both to act and not to act—are rooted in something other than love.

Love Is Not...

I would be remiss if I didn't remind us, My Dear Readers, that the reason why Matt and I wrote this book is because we have been seeing a lack of love in the virtual and in-person spaces Christians occupy and create.

With that in mind, let's first go back to one of our words for love that is particularly ripe for misuse: *eros*. Song of Songs shows us the mutuality and flourishing that *eros* should bring about, but the rest of the Bible shows us the concept of *eros* devolved: adultery, concubines, rape, prostitution. Even though the word *eros* doesn't appear in the Bible, I mention it here because the church and Christians are no strangers to creating rules and boundaries around sex and sexuality.

When we talk about sexual desire and sexuality, we need to remember that theology is not absent of bias or a cultural lens. The evangelical church is no stranger to conversations about sexuality, but a failure to acknowledge bias and power dynamics has resulted in some confusing and deeply harmful teaching. Failure to consider the generational and communal impacts of such teaching continues to reverberate through the evangelical church, with multiple scandals being revealed within churches, denominations, and Christian higher education. The #MeToo movement gave space for #ChurchToo to bring to light sexual abuse in the evangelical world.

And this abuse of power, this failure to love, goes far beyond our distortion of *eros*. My husband and I had to leave our local church of more than a decade because we were asked to tolerate racism as our expression of love. No one ever said it that way to our faces. I would have appreciated a blunt, honest, face-to-face conversation about what we, one of only a few families of color in the church, would have to tolerate in the name of love. It would've helped and sped up the process. Instead, several national events—including the mass shooting at Emanuel AME church in Charleston, South Carolina, and the very public march of white supremacists in Charlottesville, Virginia—happened with no clear response from the pulpit. There were general words about tragedies, but in between the choir-led hymns and the band-led contemporary worship songs and the announcements, no one named racism, let alone condemned it. The message was that to be loved and to love in that congregation was to value the comfort of others who were not ready to address racism.

Christians have been behind some of the most unloving cultural norms: enslaving Black people, forbidding people to marry outside of their "race" (race is a social construct, by the way), sending Indigenous children to government-funded and church-operated boarding schools to erase their culture and, as we continue to learn, in some cases murder them. Christians are not the only ones who have used the banner of religion for conquest, but it says something that the word *crusade*—specifically the mass slaughter of men, women, and children of other religions—has only recently fallen out of favor in conservative Christian circles.

Ableism is another way Christians have systemically failed to love. Did you know that religious entities are exempt from the Americans with Disabilities Act (ADA)? The Association of Christian Schools International and the National Association of Evangelicals opposed the ADA.[9] No other religions made public arguments against the ADA. Christians stand alone.

We're not calling things "crusades" anymore, and some churches are trying to be more accessible to people with disabilities. But changing a name or doing an accessibility audit on your church building doesn't erase history. Love isn't meant to erase wrongs but to heal them. If

Christians can't do out of love what secular businesses are required to do, we have no business trying to change the world.

The Universal Spiritual Gift of Love

Most often—maybe too often—1 Corinthians 13 is used in wedding ceremonies as a reminder to the couple and maybe to the attendees that love is supposed to be the answer to any disagreements or adversity the couple might face. But given the general state of the world (not to mention the fact that divorce rates among Christians aren't significantly lower than among non-Christians), maybe we should be studying the love chapter more in-depth outside of weddings.

As we learn in 1 Corinthians 13, love is and isn't a lot of things. It is patient, is kind, isn't jealous, doesn't brag, isn't arrogant, isn't rude, doesn't seek its own advantage, isn't irritable, doesn't keep record of complaints, isn't happy with injustice, and is happy with truth. Love puts up with all things and trusts all things and hopes for all things and endures all things.

I am not capable of this. Just today in the hours I've spent writing, I have not been patient, and I'm cranky (you would've been annoyed at the state of my kitchen too). I also remembered that thing my husband, Peter, promised to do almost twenty years ago and never did. I am angry about the news of another Black man being shot to death by law enforcement, but I am not up for putting up with, trusting, hoping for, and enduring much of anything today, let alone all things. Yet I am still a Christian, always invited—and sometimes compelled—to act with love.

Love is a universal spiritual gift, pulled in and through every other part of the fruit of the Spirit. It is a calling for every follower of Jesus, a way we bear the image of God, who is love.[10] And love doesn't take just one expression. People within and outside the church celebrate love through rituals and holidays, spoken words and physical expressions, in shapes and ways that transcend a particular language or culture.

I think a lot about what love looks like having grown up bicultural. My parents would learn about American customs and adopt some but not others. Letting me sleep over at a stranger's house was a big no, but they did allow me to have sleepovers with friends at our house. My parents always threw me and my sister small birthday parties, and they even bought me a corsage with sugar cubes to celebrate my sweet sixteenth birthday. But the way they really express their love? They always ask, "Have you eaten?" Even when I came down with COVID-19 during the writing of this project, they dropped off food on the doorstep of my home, an hour away from theirs.

My parents' expressions of love are unique to them and to their cultural background and personalities, which is true for all of us. However we choose to express our love, as followers of Christ, who is love, it's important that we do so.

So what do you do if you are like me, an imperfect Christian who wants to be loving and be loved in a world and in communities and in relationships where love takes many different forms and tension and disagreement and pain run rampant?

The beginning of 1 Corinthians 13 shows us that as well-meaning Christians, we can be doing a lot of things and still not be loving. This includes speaking in tongues, prophesying, moving mountains with the power of faith, and giving away our possessions. All that sounds very Christian and exactly like the things Christians should be doing, but Paul makes it clear that we can be doing things that are spiritual, even religious, and still be acting without love.

That means our intentions do matter, which is confusing in a cultural moment where the focus is on how our actions are received. Does that mean we don't have to care about how a person receives our actions so long as our intentions are good? Well, no. What Paul is pushing us to consider isn't just claiming our intentions as good but as loving, which means the person on the receiving end should experience our behavior as loving. Otherwise, as *The Message* puts it, "If I speak with human eloquence and angelic ecstasy but don't love, I'm nothing but the creaking of a rusty gate."[11] Other Bible translations equate this lack of love to noisy gongs and clanging cymbals.[12] Our spiritual actions toward others mean nothing without love. Nothing.

This clanging and noise could be a nod to pagan worship, comparing our empty religious behavior to something equally void of meaning, but even as noise alone, a rusty gate and clanging are not only annoying but can be damaging over time. I just spent three days at a music festival at which I realized—too late—that I should've worn earplugs. It's two days later, and the ringing in my ears has finally stopped, but the damage may be irreparable. What, then, is the actual witness of churches and Christian leaders who put on a show-stopping performance on Sundays but fail to protect and bring about justice for people who have experienced violence? All that noise and clanging mean nothing. Instead of inviting people to Jesus, the noise and circus turn people away.

I think about this a lot when I hop on my computer or phone. I spend a good amount of time in social-media spaces, and I pray and pause before I post, whether it's original content, responding to someone else, or elevating someone else's work. There is so much content out there, so much noise, and so much of it can do a great deal of harm. We may be "liking" posts as a way of encouragement, but the entire system has been created to manipulate our emotions, inflate our sense of value and power, and push certain narratives. Entering social media as a Christian means we enter first with love, or we bow out—even when we have the best comeback or tweetable quote.

I think about Jesus commanding us to love our neighbor[13] and how much time I spend dissecting *Who does Jesus really mean is my neighbor?* instead of carrying myself into the public sphere so that what is obvious is my love instead of my religious or political label.

What a shame if the people of God are simply known as religious and noisy. Instead of reading 1 Corinthians 13 as a pretty way to talk to newlyweds about unfailing love, what if we consistently turned to those words to remind ourselves and our communities to be more loving with those we vehemently disagree with? What if, instead of starting off with judgment about our different opinions, we led with love, just as Jesus did?

Matt

As I read this chapter, I started thinking more about how often we say that the most important commandment is to love God, and how the second is to love others. Jesus said that, so we know it's true.

Practically, though, I've experienced a sort of flattening of this saying, a way that people can in one breath quote the Scripture and in the next keep treating people with cruelty. This is usually accomplished by focusing on the "love the Lord your God" part to the exclusion of the "love your neighbor" part.

How we do this, typically, is by considering our neighbor to be in opposition to God somehow. In other words, we think we're allowed to be cruel, mean-spirited, angry, divisive toward them because of our love for God. *They're against God or God's desires, and therefore I am against them*, we tell ourselves.

This could be something as small as disagreeing with how someone dresses or something important, like a theological disagreement. t could be, and often is, politics—we've all seen plenty of unloving comments made by Christians toward politicians we don't like (or their supporters).

Two things I realized as I looked more carefully at the Galatians passage Kathy and I are reflecting on throughout this book: One, this is precisely the context in which that Paul ends up telling us about the fruit of the Spirit. He's talking to believers who are fighting each other, snapping at each other, biting each other. He warns them to be careful or they'll "devour each other."[14] Two, Paul says the entire law can be fulfilled with a single command.[15] You would think it would be "love God," right? No.

Paul says the whole law hangs on "love your neighbor as yourself." We literally cannot follow God's will if we fail to love others.

But even knowing that . . . I find it really challenging to love certain people—even whole groups of people. Kathy, do you have any thoughts about how I can grow in love toward people I find the most challenging?

Kathy

This may sound harsh, but I can learn to love people—even whole groups of people—with whom I have deep disagreements . . . and never spend time socializing with them. An extreme example would be a group of locals I've interacted with on a neighborhood Facebook page. I know their names and recognize them from the years our children attended school together. I can want the best for them and their families, which helps me remember that God sees them as much as God sees me, while also deciding that spending time in their presence would not be good for either of us. Sometimes healthy boundaries are a form of love.

Sometimes when we struggle to love people, we act out of the misunderstanding that love means some kind of direct connection, and we actually move into unloving behaviors like superficiality and avoidance. I am still learning how toxic superficial expressions of love are for true understanding and affection. I try to avoid empty offers to keep in touch or get together. I try to avoid offering help when I know I don't really mean to follow through. When a friend came down with COVID-19, instead of asking her if she needed anything, which is a kind question but not necessarily an act of love, I asked her if sending a meal via a delivery service or sending an electronic gift card would be helpful. I also try to avoid using empty platitudes you might assume have some biblical basis but don't. *God helps those who help themselves! What doesn't kill you makes you stronger! Let go and let God!* And my personal favorite: *Jesus only wept once.* (Yes, I've heard that.)

But we also need to really ask ourselves what the root of our discomfort or difficulty loving is—and whether it's something requiring boundaries, or whether we need to ask more questions. I've found that ignorance, prejudices, and insecurities can keep us from truly understanding individuals and groups of people. For example, I had built an entire narrative around why a person had not included me and my family in certain social gatherings, only to learn that the reality was they didn't have our contact information, and we were rarely home when these impromptu invitations were happening via a wave from the driveway.

Matt

Wow. That's really helpful. Okay, I have more questions from this chapter, though. I was really struck by the thought of "a different kind of love . . . a relationship based on mutuality, love focused on the pleasure and flourishing of the other and not on power and shame." (And surprised that *eros* isn't in Scripture, given that it was talked about a lot in my Christian upbringing!) But tell me this: How can a relationship focused on the pleasure of the other keep people in line? Like, if I'm focused on the pleasure of other people, couldn't that lead them toward sin instead of toward Christ?

Kathy

Whew. It's a strange relief to know that I'm not the only one programmed to associate pleasure with sin. (Maybe the word *joy* instead of *pleasure* would help those of us who are disentangling our faith in Jesus from legalism.) But our role in any relationship is not to keep other people in line. Christians are not supposed to see ourselves as the ultimate rule makers and rule enforcers. I suppose that is where we get into trouble—we assume that somehow we are fully responsible for someone else's actions. But I can't make someone sin any more than I can make someone become a Christian.

When I think about what I hope are my purest expressions of love, I automatically think about my children and closest friends. I may be too focused on what brings my children pleasure, but I also find that it expands my world to notice the things around me that maybe I don't care for or care much about but bring great joy and pleasure to my friends and family.

For example, one of my kids and a close friend are ARMY. For those of you unfamiliar with the term, it's the massive fan base of BTS, the internationally known K-pop group. I enjoy BTS's music and global impact, yet I wouldn't consider myself ARMY. But when I read about BTS in the news, I forward links, and most recently someone I follow on Etsy made keychains and hair scrunchies out of fabric with the faces of BTS members, so naturally I made a purchase. Why? Because the delight in the faces of those I love makes my heart explode. That's what I mean by focusing on others.

I am also aware that being too focused on the joy and pleasure of other people can become toxic, people pleasing, and manipulative. In my worst parenting moments, I've used bribery—*I'll give you this thing you want if you clean your room.* There is a place and time and stage of parenting and child development for incentivizing behavior, but it should never become a replacement for a relationship that's based on mutual love.

It's also important to remember I see love in mutuality—in seeing each other as equals. As someone who once received free breakfast and lunches at school, I've seen the ugly side of charity and a "love" that tells someone they are a project. That's why it's important that many local food banks have redesigned their programs to honor the dignity of clients. Instead of handing someone a bag of food put together by a volunteer, food banks resemble grocery stores so that clients experiencing food insecurity can take what they need instead of having someone imply, "Be grateful for whatever we give you."

Matt

You say our love, instead of our religion, must lead. But isn't it loving to tell people about Jesus?

Kathy

If someone asks me about my personal beliefs or faith practices, sure. I'm happy to tell them about Jesus, but that's never my opening line. I do hope that our actions, the way we engage with the world, are beautiful and challenge the status quo. Our lives should draw people into a curiosity about our beliefs, and that can lead to a conversation about Jesus.

I'm beginning to see that the emphasis on the recitation of something akin to the Sinner's Prayer or a public proclamation of Jesus articulated verbally between individuals or to a group of people is a uniquely modern white evangelical thing. (Am I wrong?) The lived witness—the Good News—comes first. If my life or the life of my faith community is harmful to the broader community, a public proclamation of my faith and the label of "Christian" is obnoxious and hypocritical.

CHAPTER 3

JOY AND HAPPINESS

Happiness Is Easier Because It Has an *I*

Kathy

I SPENT MY FIRST DECADE OF LIFE in the Korean immigrant church. Sundays were completely immersed in familiar smells of barley tea and savory soups and broths—so much better than coffee hour, My Dear Readers—and the sounds of Korean and English. I first learned to sing hymns in Korean, not always understanding the words I was singing.

And then came the Sunday school teachers—most often non-Korean, white seminary students fulfilling internship requirements. They taught me and a generation of immigrant church kids Christian choruses and camp songs like "I've got the joy, joy, joy, joy down in my heart."

I bet you can finish that stanza.

I'm also a child of the eighties, so when I think of the word *joy*, my brain plays the first two lines from Rob Base and DJ E-Z Rock's hit song: "Joy and pain / Like sunshine and rain."[1] Between those two songs is some good, basic theology to help us understand the difference and connection between joy and happiness—because only one of those two can help us create a more loving community.

Same? Not Same

Isn't joy the same thing as happiness? Yes and no.

Language is a funny thing. Various sources describe both joy and happiness as a feeling or emotion we experience. The *Oxford English Dictionary* defines *joy* as "the feeling or state of being highly pleased or delighted" and *happy* as "feeling or showing a deep sense of pleasure or contentment."[2] *Merriam-Webster* defines *joy* as "the emotion evoked by well-being, success, or good fortune" and "a state of happiness or felicity," and *happiness* as "a state of well-being and contentment."[3]

I got stuck while writing this chapter because of this never-ending feedback loop between joy and happiness. These two emotions and experiences are intrinsically connected, yet they have come to mean different things in the way we use the words.

Happiness is an individualized emotion that comes and goes depending on external circumstances. But joy, based on what we see in the Bible,[4] is a deep knowing and understanding of God's goodness and grace for us. Joy connects us not only to God but to one another's well-being.

Happiness can be easier to achieve than joy because it focuses on what pleases you or me as an individual. I think happiness is in some ways the most American emotion because it is so individualistic. Happiness is about *I* and has nothing to do with *us*. Just watch two little kids playing with a toy. One kid takes the toy away from the other. One cries and one is happy until an adult comes around with a reprimand and admonishment to share. At that age, sharing does not necessarily bring happiness. But hopefully as adults, as we learn to share not only out of our abundance but also in times of what we may experience as scarcity, we will have learned to cultivate both happiness *and* joy.

Without that balance, the single-minded pursuit of happiness quickly turns toxic. Women are accosted on the street and told to "smile."[5] (Don't do it, folks. Just don't.) Parents or other adults tell children or one another to stop crying. We are trained to perform happiness and be uncomfortable with discomfort, unhappiness, or displeasure—anything that indicates the external world is amiss and that that has impacted our inner world.

Based on unscientific observations at my two favorite thrift stores, the days of "Blessed" signs are numbered, but that isn't to say toxic positivity in faith circles has gone the way of shabby chic décor. Even as church leaders and Christian influencers discuss the merits of and need for authenticity, the reality we experience in Christian settings is too often a facade of Sunday best.

Christians should push against toxic positivity because it is not honest or true. Sure, that kind of language and outlook may seem benign. After all, what is the harm in trying to encourage someone to look on the bright side? Well, sometimes there is no bright side. We live in a broken world with systems created by broken people. Sure, someone can remind you that your loved one is in heaven with Jesus, and that's true. But toxic positivity tells you that grief should look a certain way and last an acceptable amount of time because there is a happy ever after and your grief makes other people uncomfortable. The thing is grief isn't linear or convenient. Encouraging others to maintain an "everything is fine" facade has helped normalize racism and sexism and a host of other hateful behaviors, all to keep the peace.

A local family was in a fatal head-on collision—the mother, her four children, and a thirteen-year-old passenger died at the scene, and the father was airlifted to a hospital. When the father died three days later, news coverage proclaimed the man had received his "angel wings."[6] Social-media comments included several on the theme of God deciding it was better that the father join his family in heaven than survive the crash. But what kind of higher power decides it's better for an entire family to die from the same tragic event than for any one person to survive? Dear Christian, does that same silver lining work in reverse? When the parents of a toddler are killed in a mass shooting, would we say it would be better if the child had also died? I hope not. But that is what toxic positivity does. It is uncomfortable with the harsh and broken realities of the world. It looks for an easy out to explain something unexplainable. When happiness is our only goal or our higher value, toxic positivity tries to drown out the silence and reality of suffering.

This isn't to say happiness isn't important, but it isn't the most important thing in life. It's better to learn to sit with discomfort and hold things in tension than to pursue happiness as the ultimate goal. Individual happiness can't fulfill you. Happiness can't sit in the inherently complicated tension of community. But joy can. Joy can hold beauty and pain in one single breath and help carve part of a path for how to be in community and bear difficult things together.

You can't avoid disagreements when you are in a community whose members are allowed to be authentic, to acknowledge what they're actually feeling, and to be fully human. But joy gives each of us an opportunity to live beyond our individual comfort and find something richer in the depths.

Finding Joy in the Depths

I have anxiety and depression. I've been on medication for more than a decade, under the care of a doctor, and I have gone through several rounds of therapy with a licensed therapist. I have come to understand that my depression is a part of who I am, just like my cultural identity is a part of who I am.

Depression, however, can overwhelm me. While tools like medication and therapy help keep me from despair or the inability to fully function or self-harm, depression also pushes me to wrestle with the differences between joy and happiness—because what keeps me alive is not happiness but joy. When I feel the weight of depression, I cannot cheer myself out of it. My friends and family cannot constantly create circumstances that satisfy some sort of need or craving. My favorite deep-dish buttercrust pizza cannot snap me out of depression, even if it brings me a moment of happiness.

I am not dismissing happiness, nor am I saying that you can self-help your way out of depression. But I am saying that depression has unexpectedly been the invitation to cultivate and live into joy, to choose and even search for joy amid the ups and downs of fleeting happiness. And I have found that even in the depths of depression, there is so much grace.

In Galatians 5:22, the word translated as "joy" is *chara* (χαρά), derived from the Greek word *charis*, meaning "grace." Without grace, we cannot experience joy, and as Christians we understand that we cannot experience true grace without God. Why is that? Because grace is simply God's love. We may not always or often attribute our joy to God or even acknowledge God's presence as we experience joy, but joy cannot be separated from God.

We express joy through rejoicing. In the Bible, *chairō* (χαίρω), commonly translated *rejoice*, means "favorably disposed"; "leaning towards [God's grace]."[7] Rejoicing is living in God's grace. I continue to learn that living in God's grace, rejoicing in the Lord always,[8] is not about being perpetually happy. To rejoice is to lean toward God just like a plant leans toward the sun, absorbs the energy, processes carbon dioxide, and releases oxygen, which we humans need to survive. When I lean into God's grace, the result should be not for my own benefit but for the benefit of others. To live out joy is to allow God's grace to transform us and the way we react to and interact with everything around us, including people with whom we disagree.

Culturally and personality-wise, I can appreciate the nuances of experiencing and expressing joy in ways that are not perceived as happiness but are perhaps closer to contentment or peace. Yes, I know. Peace is another fruit of the Spirit and yet very much a part of joy, which is very much a part of love. The fruit of the Spirit is a bit like God, Jesus, and the Spirit in the Trinity—separate and one, distinct but inseparable.

While I can be rather effusive in my facial expressions, my immigrant parents are often read by white Americans as reserved. In fact, smiling is not a universal expression of happiness and joy. My parents' generation of Koreans weren't taught or told to smile for the camera. But their joy is deep and holds love and disappointment in tension.

I can't help but think of my mom's dresses. When my parents married, my father's parents gifted my mother yards of beautiful silk to be made into clothing for her new married life. Because my parents had planned to emigrate to the United States, my mom had two dresses and two coats custom made—party dresses for the incredible life she imagined ahead. Then those dresses sat in her closet unworn, collecting dust for more than two decades until I asked to have them.

I wore the emerald-green A-line dress and matching coat for my naturalization ceremony and again for the only time I was asked to speak in front of my Asian American ministry colleagues. I wore the coral-pink dress for a friend's engagement party. When I told my mother I was wearing her dresses, she didn't jump up and down in excitement or ask to see pictures. She expressed her joy by telling me the story of how those dresses came to be, how they sat in her closet, and how she never imagined they would not be worn until finally put on by her daughter, who was living the life she had hoped to live.

There was sadness in her voice and expression but also an amazement and leaning toward God, who had walked with her in her fifty-plus years in the United States. There were so many losses in those years, but that is how joy deepens: time. Her joy held in tension the disappointments for what would never be, the hope for what still could be, and the gratitude for what is.

My parents and I have had several deep disagreements over the years, some of which have created long silences in our relationship. One of those periods of silence was broken by my father, who said my parents did not want to dwell on our differences of opinion and beliefs. That desire wasn't about changing anyone's beliefs. He said they wanted to live their lives in joy. For years I believed they wanted to ignore the schism and pretend it hadn't happened (well, maybe that's a little true), but when I think back to my dad's words, I am humbled. He was saying he wanted to choose a joy that runs deep, rather than let a relationship be broken. That kind of joy allows us and fuels us to live in a broken world.

Joy for the World

Joy connects us not only to the God who loves us but also to the well-being of each person around us. Viruses, after all, are not the only contagions in the world—emotions are contagious. I teach yoga, and you'll hear yoga teachers and others in the wellness industry say things about "bad" energy and "good" energy. My Sunday school sensibilities always used to shut that down—but then I would sit down in the pews and notice that when we sang songs of celebration, joy would spread. Sure, not everyone clapped because that wasn't the cultural tradition and expression, but you would see folks swaying, little kids dancing, and I would be clapping. There is some research around how we pick up and mimic the emotions of those around us.[9] My joy can actually help shift someone else's emotional state.

When we can see ourselves connected to one another, as a body, we are a step closer to understanding how every other person's joy is a reminder to me of God's goodness, which should bring me joy. We are connected because of God and through God. God doesn't love just me or you. God loves the world. That is why we must be careful to not focus solely on grace and joy as God's love for you or me individually. God so loved the world that Jesus, God's only Son, was given to *the world*[10]—not just to separate individuals.

The idea that we are connected to one another, that our well-being is connected to others', can be uncomfortable for many Christians who grew up believing the primary reason for putting your faith in Jesus is for your individual salvation. Somewhere someone told us to replace "the world" with "me" to make God's love personal, emphasizing and elevating an individualistic experience of the gospel and the fruit of the Spirit. That individualistic theology aligns well with myopic concepts such as American exceptionalism and our "pull yourself up by your bootstraps" mentality. But no one—absolutely no one—achieves anything in life without some help from others, whether systems, people, or God. Yes, God loves you and me as individuals, but that isn't what makes God's love, his grace, radical. God LOVES ALL OF US. Even the people—especially the people—you and I don't love, which is also why bearing the fruit of the Spirit is so hard. My most basic instincts often are not Christlike. My natural state is not inclusive but exclusive.

That is our invitation in loving disagreement: to be more like God and enter the joy of others as a way forward. Instead of leading with a fight, how might we lead with what connects us as a community? If our disagreement is between Christians, how can sharing in one another's joy help us ease back into the fight in a way that seeks the well-being of the whole community?

When I am teaching yoga, I sometimes cue a pose that may create some discomfort, so I tell students to use their breath as a pause. Pause, identify the place of discomfort, and then slowly back out of the pose with an inhale. When the class is ready to ease back into the pose, I invite them to reengage with an exhale. What if we did the same when we are in a disagreement? What if we took time to identify and name the places of discomfort (maybe taking several deep breaths)—and then, with the discomfort attended to, shift our focus to places of common joy to ease out of the discomfort of disagreement before reengaging?

The discipline of awareness and leaning toward God's grace to every single one of us is, I have found, an invitation into community—the place where we are known and know, are loved and love. We will not find a way forward independent of one another.

An exhortation from Philippians 4:4 comes to mind: "Rejoice in the Lord always. I will say it again: Rejoice!" What I love about the song based on that verse is that it is sung in a round, the lyrics and voices overlapping, sometimes in harmony. The words keep repeating, never-ending, overflowing, much like God's grace. And so it is with our joy. As we lean toward God's grace, as we choose joy for the benefit of each other, we find ourselves singing joy in chorus, our voices overlapping and overflowing, weaving together threads of reminders of God's goodness.

I mentioned that I ran into some major writer's block with this chapter. Instead of typing and deleting random thoughts, I jumped on Twitter to ask others what brings them joy. And guess what? Reading the responses brought me joy. A smile came to my face as I imagined each one of my Twitter friends sitting in joy. Let me invite you, My Dear Readers, to sit with me and imagine friends . . .

- watching bees gather pollen
- drawing
- writing
- talking with a friend, commiserating about painful things
- landing that hard skateboard trick after many failed tries
- eating breakfast with their grandson
- working with people they love on a meaningful project

- seeing people they love
- creating a garden or beautiful space to share
- seeing their kids' love for each other
- enjoying the smell of fall
- spending long hours on the beach in the Caribbean
- eating anything that reminds them of home
- seeing somebody really flourish after a setback
- watching blooming flowers in the garden

It's worth noting that these responses weren't centered on things you can buy (though some of them cost money at some point). But you get the idea, I hope, that joy is not found in things but in relationship with one another and with the natural world around us. It is found in our experiences—with friends or with a hobby or new skill—that connect us to one another, to creation, and to God. Joy cannot be bought but it can be shared and multiplied, and that should be part of the Good News in a world where division between the haves and the have-nots grows deeper and wider every day.

Matt

Can you talk a little bit about the difference between joy and "triumphalism"? I've been in churches that refuse to acknowledge anything negative, whether in the community or in an individual's life . . . but that's not true joy, right?

Kathy

You're right. That's not joy. That's pretending to be perfect, and I suspect all churches and cultures wrestle with being fully honest, not only individually but also collectively. I don't think any of us enjoy having our dirty laundry aired publicly, but pretending everything is always celebratory and wonderful is a false gospel. Good News doesn't mean things are perfect. Good News means that when you are grieving, the community will walk with you, maybe even carry you. And remember that we can be joyful *and* hold in tension grief and loss.

Some of the most beautiful expressions of a church community coming together have been in times of loss. Instead of an officiant using the opportunity to scare people into a come-to-Jesus moment—and I've seen those—pastors have named the pain and loss of losing a loved one, encouraged laughter and joy as stories are shared, and allowed the hard questions to remain unanswered but acknowledged as part of the experience. Being allowed to experience the fullness of our humanity is a joy.

Triumphalism shows up when the church and Christians think we are the best—the best at loving, the best at being faithful, the best at "you name it." To my non-Christian and non-religious friends, that just comes off as arrogance and not as celebratory or joyful. It also comes off as a disconnect when Christians want to claim our faith is "the best" but are uncomfortable with the complexity of real life. We've all seen others deal with this discomfort or have experienced it ourselves. I was thirteen weeks pregnant when we learned there would be no baby. Well-meaning friends, many of whom were Christians, told me to be thankful that I already had a healthy child, reminded me I was still young and could try for another baby, and told me that the loss was God's way of protecting me and Peter from having a child with disabilities or health problems. None of those comments helped. What helped was when my two-year-old daughter carefully crawled into my lap, wiped away my tears with her sticky hands, and said, "Mommy's sad." I can still feel her body on mine (which is weird since she's now twenty-seven) and that experience of joy and grief.

Matt

I've honestly experienced a lot of joy in church during potlucks and food gatherings. Many Korean churches have food every week after services, and so did some of the Baptist churches I attended as a kid. Do you think there's a connection there? And if you and I ever meet in person, we're going to get some Korean food, right?

Kathy

If we meet in person, we will definitely get food, but the kind of food will depend on where we meet up.

And yes to the connection of joy (and love) and food, especially in the context of potlucks and gatherings. The loss of that tradition of gathering for a meal during the COVID-19 pandemic has been challenging for many congregations and families. While I am a firm believer in keeping virtual options for worship in place, I know that not gathering physically for meals with friends negatively impacted my well-being.

In Korean churches, there is an abundance of food. In other areas of the culture there may be a frugality, but that frugality and the abundance and generosity of food and hospitality both come from places of deep loss and pain from colonization and war and freedom. We all have our favorite foods that are connected to people, places, and experiences. The smells and tastes bring us back into the memories, some bittersweet. But there is always a sense of joy, a sense of abiding with God, when we are in the company of others and see our universal physical need for food mct.

What I have had to remind myself of is that the amount or type of food is not the ultimate expression of joy. It is in the gathering of people.

CHAPTER 4

FIGHTING FOR PEACE

The World as It Should Be

Matt

YEARS AGO I WAS RUNNING a Christian conference in the mountains of Colorado. Several hundred recent college grads attended, all headed overseas as missionaries. Participants came from across the US, some who had been Christian their whole lives and some who had come to Christ in college.

It was August, and we had rented out a large portion of a ski resort (a relatively cheap option in the off season). There was one other large gathering there with us: a Hasidic Jewish group, made up of young people about the same age as ours. Hasidic Judaism is committed to what some call "ultra orthodox" Jewish faith. There are a variety of rules related to how to dress, what to eat, how to observe the Sabbath, et cetera.

As you can imagine, our groups had some differences of opinions on a variety of topics. Mostly that was okay—we shared some common spaces, but we were all doing our own thing. However, there were a few sticking points, and the leader of their conference and I got together to talk about it.

His name was Eli, and the two of us got along great. Our main conversation was "How can we all get along and share this space with the minimum of conflict?" Eli identified a handful of things that were causing them some dismay, and he came with solutions in mind. Our expectations of how women should dress were drastically different (Hasidic Jewish women cover their knees and elbows as well as their hair; the women in our group were wearing shorts and T-shirts); Eli wanted us to use a side door so his folks didn't have to see ours. Their group wanted to cover all our TVs and computers with cloth for the Sabbath (in case someone happened to look in the direction of our space). And in hang-out areas, they wanted only one kind of music playing: Hasidic Jewish rap ("You students like rap, right?").

To complicate things even further, many of the Hasidic youth had never been outside their own Hasidic neighborhood in Brooklyn, so for some of them this was the first time they had interacted with anyone who wasn't Jewish. On the flip side, I was pretty sure none of these young Christian twentysomethings had ever hung out with any Hasidic Jews.

So what was to be done? Eli and I both shared what we needed and wanted from each other, and it was clear we weren't going to come to a mutually satisfying conclusion. I wasn't going to have the women in our group coming in and out of our building through a side door. It wasn't an option to cut off internet access for a day for our participants (they were leaving the country the next day and needed to check in for flights and contact parents and so on). But even so, Eli and I eventually came to a place of peace, in the sense that we no longer had conflict. We'd laid all our needs out on the table and knew and understood each other's positions. My conference talked to our participants about the situation, and Eli even shared some tips about how to interact respectfully with his group. Overall, we ended up with no big issues and coexisted quite nicely.

There was one interesting moment, though. I was out walking on the mountain and crossed paths with an older rabbi who was there to teach in Eli's group. As I passed him, I nodded and said, "Shalom." *Shalom* is the Hebrew word for "peace," and it's a common greeting and farewell in Jewish circles, especially Orthodox Judaism. It's a wish of peace to another person, and usually the response is to say "Shalom" in return.

The rabbi looked at me very carefully, nodded, and then said, "Thank you." Huh. That was weird. I wasn't sure of what to make of it. I saw Eli later that day and asked him about it.

Eli's first theory was that sometimes Jewish people get annoyed when Christians want to "bond" over their "shared faith" and try to show off that they know something about Judaism. We agreed that could be it but also that it seemed unlikely after a single "Shalom." We talked more about the guy until Eli had a pretty good guess who I'd seen.

"Oh, that guy," he said. "I know what was happening there. He didn't wish you shalom because shalom might not be so good for you."

Wait, what? How could peace not be good for me?

Eli explained that shalom usually means something much more than an "absence of conflict." Shalom means "the world as it should be." Or, to say it in explicitly Christian terms, "Your will be done on earth as it is in heaven."

Okay, so shalom meant an absence of conflict that came about because the world had been put right. Everything as it should be. No injustice, nothing to be angry about, nothing to fight over.

"It sounds pretty good to me," I said. "Why wouldn't I want that?"

Eli grinned at me.

"Well, for one thing," he said, "you'd have to cover up those computer screens on Saturday."

The World as It Should Be

When God finally puts everything to right and repairs the world, Eli explained, then we'll truly have shalom. But inherent in the idea of true peace, of shalom, is the idea that the coming of shalom may not be universally accepted as a good thing. Some people won't like it because it'll mean that they have to change their behavior or that they'll face judgment or that the gains other people make in the movement toward peace will be losses for them.

Let's imagine a man who has become wealthy by harming people around him. He's overworking and underpaying his employees. In fact, he's even skimming money that belongs to the employees—taking their retirement, maybe. The coming of shalom will be a great thing for his workers but not so great for him. In a shalom world, people won't be hungry, and there won't be injustice. Shalom requires that everyone will be taken care of, that every person will have what they need.

Achieving shalom will require that we radically alter the way we look at wealth. And it will certainly require we do away with sinful uses of wealth or sinful ways of acquiring wealth. Will this greedy employer welcome the coming of shalom with open arms? Almost certainly not. Shalom will mean a loss for him. As the world is set right, what has been stolen will need to be repaid. Those who have lost money to him will need it restored. He could very well be bankrupted and find himself living much like his employees. It wouldn't be a surprise if—though his employees are grateful for shalom—he is bitter about it.

I suspect that, even in that example, some readers might be chafing and feeling uncomfortable. *Sounds like socialism*, someone might be thinking. (And it's fair to ask questions about redistribution of wealth. Although the whole idea of shalom is that "all is as it should be," how do we make sure such a redistribution is just and doesn't create more problems?) If we were sitting in a room together somewhere, this story might spark a conversation between us—or maybe even an argument. We might disagree about how to go about things.

So let's talk about an easier topic. How about gun control in the United States?

Okay, I'm joking. (Someone probably just put their copy of this book into a bonfire.) Guns in the US is a huge, emotionally fraught topic. If you want to see some Christians not acting "civil" and definitely not behaving like they have the fruit of the Spirit, just get a few of them who disagree in a room and ask them how we should deal with school shootings. Sparks (and probably tempers and possibly fists) will fly.

But why?

I think because we are focused on peace as the absence of conflict instead of as the world as it should be. We get frustrated in these conversations where we disagree because, we think, *We're in the family of God. We shouldn't be having this kind of conflict.* So we're tempted to disassociate from one another, to argue someone into agreement with us, or to avoid really important problems. That's not peace; that's an illusion of peace.

What may be more helpful is for us to describe together the world of shalom. Everyone—every single one of us—agrees that in the world-that-should-be, children wouldn't be killed by guns, whether in school shootings, accidents, war, or as victims of suicide. No one wants that. Every person I know, certainly every Christian I know, would agree with that. We collectively long for a world where zero children are killed by guns.

That is an astonishing amount of common ground, and we often toss it all aside when we start talking tactics and politics. And we should also be able to agree on this: Scripture is clear that a time is coming when there will be no more weapons. Swords will be beaten into plowshares. No one will die from battle or be harmed by swords or guns or bombs or any other weapon.[1]

"But that's completely naive," some will say (and have said to me). "We can't do away with every single gun. What about the Second

Amendment? What about the fact that we live in a broken world, not yet in God's Kingdom? There are other things to consider here!"

That's true.

But it would be wise for us to remember that when we pray "Your will be done, on earth as it is in heaven," we are praying for shalom today, not in some distant future.

In Conflict over Peace

Despite our reputation at times, Christians have a long history of working toward shalom in the world. Why? Well, Galatians makes that clear: Peace is a fruit of the Spirit. If the Spirit is in our lives, we can't help but want to make the world the way it should be. That can be in small things, like bringing a meal to a neighbor who's sick, or learning to speak with kindness to people at our workplace or at church or home. It can be personal, like paying attention to places in our own hearts that are not as they should be and working to repair those.

None of that is controversial. We're not going to get in an argument about me taking minestrone soup to my neighbor. And while, yes, I once sat in a church meeting where the congregation argued over which kind of light bulbs to buy for the auditorium, I don't think anyone would object to me learning to be kinder to my children.

Shalom, though, can also be big, culture-shaping movements.

The abolitionist movement was heavily Christian in its early days, for instance. Elizabeth Heyrick, a Quaker, started the sugar boycott because she didn't think it was right to eat sugar if enslaved people were the ones producing it, and she wanted to strike at the core profitability of using slave labor. Heyrick and other Christian abolitionists in England and the United States looked at slavery and said, "This is not shalom. This is not the world as it should be. The people of Africa are also made in the image of God."

Many of the founders and influential proponents of first-wave feminism were followers of Christ: Lucretia Mott, Susan B. Anthony, Frances Willard. These were women who saw a world where women were marginalized and couldn't vote or own property or participate in a huge variety of societal structures, and who said, "This is not right." They set out to change it.

Martin Luther King Jr.'s famous "I have a dream" speech was pure shalom in motion. He was imagining the world of shalom, telling us what the world could and should be.

And there are many, many other examples we could share of Christians bringing more shalom into the world, from Mother Teresa working among the poor to Frank Laubach seeking to eradicate illiteracy globally.

I'm guessing with a few of these examples, you're already saying to yourself, *But wait, not every Christian was on the same side of these questions.* And you're right. These big, culture-shaping movements are also where we often find ourselves in conflict. There were more Christian slaveholders than Christian abolitionists at the start of the movement. There are Christians today who see feminism as something in opposition to the Kingdom, despite the Christian roots of the movement. And while we might rush to embrace Martin Luther King Jr.—which was not the case for many evangelicals when Dr. King was alive—we have to acknowledge that William Joseph Simmons is one of "ours" as well.[a]

You know, William Joseph Simmons. The guy who revived the Ku Klux Klan in 1915 and was its first Imperial Wizard. Preacher, minister, and teacher: William Joseph Simmons.

Simmons thought he was working toward shalom too. The Klan was anti-Black, anti-Semitic, anti-immigrant, and anti-Catholic. Simmons saw his organization as a theological agent designed to destroy those who prevented the world from being "as it should be."

The temptation here, of course, is to jettison someone like Simmons from the conversation. "Well, he's not a real Christian." And this may be hard to hear, but that instinct comes from our lesser definition of peace: a desire to throw out the conflict and keep a false sense of tranquility. "Of course all Christians can agree that guy was wrong." No. Nearly every member of the Klan was a Protestant Christian.[3] That's something we need to examine, not discard.

What if this is an example of a fellow citizen of heaven who has failed to adopt our heavenly culture? How do we help such a person hear from the Holy Spirit and work toward shalom rather than against it? It's complicated. This fellow citizen is doing real harm (physical, emotional, and spiritual) against others, so a simple "Let's agree to disagree" isn't sufficient. Kathy addressed in the conversation at the end of chapter 1 how white supremacy comes at a cost for everyone involved, including the white supremacist. In this example Simmons needed shalom, and so did the people he was harming. I sometimes wonder if this is why we're told to preach the Good News to one another—to help us recognize the places where our own understandings are twisted. So the question becomes: How can I best be an agent of shalom in a situation like that?

Our work toward shalom must include an honest reckoning of where we have come from and how we have gotten here, and a clear-eyed look at how we might be causing harm in the name of shalom today as well. Only then can we actively participate in making shalom together, rather than hiding in our corners of division in the name of keeping the peace.

Peacemakers, Not Peacekeepers

One of the many things I love about evangelicalism is that—at our best—we've been an activist community. In fact, scholars who study evangelicalism often identify that as a defining marker. Evangelicals have often been part of big, culture-shaping movements, pushing in and saying, "There is a better way for the world to be than this."

But why are these big, culture-shaping movements controversial? Why do they invite conflict? Because inevitably the movement toward shalom means changing things. And yes, at our best we have pushed hard for those changes. But at our worst, we've sometimes been at the forefront of resisting them. Too often our preoccupation with "keeping the peace" prevents us from working toward actual peace, toward shalom.

Jesus said, "Blessed are the peacemakers, for they will be called children of God."[4] God is one who makes peace, and if we also make peace, we are like God. Parents and children often look alike, so it's no surprise someone would look at a peacemaker and think, *That's one of God's kids.*

We are called to be peacemakers, not peacekeepers.

What's the difference?

Well, peacekeepers are defenders of the status quo. They're working to keep things as they are. Whether in war or law enforcement or the church, a peacekeeper is someone whose job is to stop conflict. There can be huge value in this, and it can even sometimes be part of peacemaking. But peacekeepers can also be a powerful force against the movement toward shalom because peacekeepers are preoccupied with "lack of conflict." Which means that if movement toward shalom is going to cause discomfort, awkwardness, trouble, conflict, or unsettled emotions, the peacekeeper is going to step in to say, "Hey, we don't need that." It's "harmony" at the expense of true peace.

An easy example of this would be the various sex- and child-abuse scandals in the church. Every time there are accusations of sex abuse in the church, there is a vocal group of people who say things like "We need to deal with this privately"—but what they mean is "We need to keep this quiet." A peacekeeper might pressure a victim to "forgive and forget" because . . . well, because this leads to a lack of conflict.

During a recent child-abuse scandal in the church, I saw a number of pastors, true followers of Jesus, who were saying publicly, "It is a stain on the witness of the church to talk about these things where nonbelievers can see them."

No! That is not shalom, and it does not move us toward shalom. Why is the focus on the reputation of the church, on pretending that abuse doesn't happen, instead of on dealing with the abuse? And working to prevent it from ever happening again?

It is a stain on the witness of the church to protect sexual abusers at the expense of people who have experienced sexual violence. It is a stain on the witness of the church to hide the wrongs abusers have done and allow those people to go to another church or to minister in another denomination. It's a stain on the witness of the church to not call the cops when a child has been harmed because "We're dealing with it in-house" or (worse) "What if this controversy destroys our church?" If protecting children will cause your church to collapse, then your church isn't built on the right foundation. In a moment like that, a peacemaker grabs a sledgehammer and gets to work.

Peacekeepers insist that we cannot critique the church. But the church is not yet what she should be. It is an act of shalom to point that out, just like it's an act of shalom to celebrate the places where the church most fully reflects the heart of God. The deep shalom of God will always push us toward making the world a better place, toward seeing God's heart for justice manifested in our systems and our communities and our relationships.

A peacemaker looks carefully at the world and asks, "Is this the way God desires the world to be?" And when they inevitably find places where it is not—in their communities, their churches, their own hearts—they roll up their sleeves and start making changes. Peacemakers are always pushing to make things better, even when conflict is a result.

The prophets were peacemakers, not peacekeepers. They weren't always liked. They didn't always live to tell about it later. But the Holy Spirit, planted deep in their hearts, led them to say, "The world is not as it should be!" And yes, the people who liked the world just the way it was strenuously objected. As citizens of heaven, we'll all encounter times when the Spirit points out things that are not as they should be and nudges us: "Hey, why don't you be the one to fix this?" That's one of the ways we bring our heavenly citizenship to our earthly location. Peacemaking is our job as ambassadors.

Where Peace and Righteousness Meet

I know all this peacemaking and prophet talk could sound like an invitation to cruelty. It might sound like I'm saying, "All conflict is godly and should be encouraged." Or it might sound like an encouragement to that certain type of person in your church who always has a dramatic complaint to make about things not going their way. Not at all. Christ tells us that people will know we are God's followers by our love for each other.[5] And when Jesus was asked which law of God was the most important, he said love for God and love for each other. In fact, he said all the law could be followed just by following those two core commands.[6] Everything else hangs on love.

And as Kathy so wisely noted, love is the universal spiritual gift for believers. We Christians are "always invited—and sometimes compelled—to act with love."

The movement toward shalom must be motivated by our love for others. We don't seek peace for peace's sake but because the world of shalom is a better world for the people around us. And how do we tell which side to take on thorny questions in our culture? Well, we won't go wrong by choosing the most loving side of the question.[7]

Psalm 85:10 says, "Love and faithfulness meet together; righteousness and peace kiss each other." Shalom always intersects with righteousness eventually, just like love and faithfulness walk hand in hand. Righteousness is simply "doing the right thing" . . . and true peace is never more than a breath away from doing what's right.

We've been talking about what it means to be true citizens of heaven even though we're "living abroad" here in the world. We're ambassadors, trying to teach other people what it means to live in our home culture, the culture of heaven. That means that, sometimes, the act of shalom may not even be fixing what's broken. Maybe it can't be fixed until Jesus sits on the throne. But at the very least, shalom is loving people enough to point out the broken places and say, "That's not right. The world should be better than that."

Shalom is the act of saying, "Come, Lord Jesus."

Shalom is the prayer, "Your will be done on earth as in heaven."

Shalom is seeing the world as it is and envisioning what it could be.

Shalom is rolling up our sleeves and getting to work.

Kathy

I find it rather odd that any Christians in the US would expect peace in our churches and communities. As a Christian, we should desire and strive for peace—be peacemakers—but war and conquest run the full course of US history. I find it hilarious when Christians tell me how uncomfortable and un-Christian it is to rock the boat. Many of us, after all, come from *Protest*ant roots.

My activism is rooted in my faith. The way I try to live out my faith is an act of protest against systems that were created without consideration for me and other people of color and for me and other women. I disagree with the notion that the United States is or ought to be a Christian nation because I do not believe a democratic system allows for Christians or any particular group to single-handedly rule over everyone else. Moreover, Christians ourselves are not somehow divinely more qualified to lead or rule. It is Jesus who is King, and his Kingdom is not of this world. He invites us to bring about God's Kingdom and do God's will on earth as it is in heaven.[8] Yes, there were some Christians involved in building this country; in broad strokes, they didn't imagine someone like me or anyone in my family to be fully human, let alone full participants in our democracy. Christians in this country also codified slavery and tried to obliterate Indigenous peoples and their cultures.

I think that is why my activism is disorienting and uncomfortable for some white Christians. The systems have been created for them, and shalom sounds great in theory when you assume you wouldn't have to change much. But shalom is for everyone, not just for a comfortable few. That's why shalom doesn't always come in the language of comfort, and why my voice can be uncomfortable and disruptive for people like you, Matt. Most often, other Christians are the ones who don't like my anger, tone, and assertiveness, and who demand or expect a certain type of deference from me. "Why are you so angry? You don't need to yell/type in all caps. Why can't we just agree to disagree? Why do you have to make this public?" Telling other people how they should and shouldn't respond to injustice isn't peacemaking. This is tone policing, which has more to do with our own discomfort with conflict than it does with actually resolving conflict.

Matt, when did you start experiencing more discomfort in the church and in this country? Were there any specific shifts externally and internally that our readers could learn from? And how do you manage that discomfort even now?

Matt

My journey in stepping out of my own comfort and living in the tension of shalom is a lot more complicated than most people might expect. I had some advantages when it came to seeing the impact of marginalization—recognizing racial injustice as well as prejudice against the LGBTQ+ community—largely because of experiences

I had when I was young. The first time I had a Black woman in authority over me was when I was in kindergarten (Mrs. Hook was my teacher for about half the year). I knew a lot of people in the gay community in the San Francisco Bay Area in the eighties and nineties (even though at that time there was little overlap with my church community).

But one of the bigger moments for me was my junior year of college. I went to UC Riverside, which at the time had a white population of 8 percent. So, for instance, I was the only white male in my hall at the dorm. Two things converged to challenge my status quo. One, for the first time I was outside the Christian bubble I had grown up in. (Church several times a week and Christian school meant that before college my "outside" relationships were sparse.) This brought to light some things I'd been taught that weren't true (e.g., "God is love and therefore people who aren't Christians can't be loving") and altered the way I saw people who weren't Christ followers. My experience revealed some holes in my theological education.

Second, as I moved into deeper relationship in communities of color in particular, I learned about prejudice, racism, and bias "firsthand" because it was impacting my friends. I was in the room for racist comments. I saw prejudice in action—directed toward my friends—when we went out places together. (This was true with my gay friends too. One of them had a brick thrown through his window in our dorm, with "anti-gay" Bible verses written in Sharpie.) It troubled me when I started realizing that my church life and my Christian school life had been so culturally in line with majority culture. Sure, not every person in my churches or schools had been white, but while I'd had a Black teacher in kindergarten, she'd been the only Black teacher I'd had in Christian school. There were people of color in nearly all my classes growing up, but usually only one or two. I started wondering why many of my diverse friends and their families consistently felt uncomfortable in the culture of my church.

The answer I arrived at was that evangelicalism has been a highly successful contextualization of Christianity, initially developing out of attempts to reach white middle- and upper-class folks with the Gospel.[9] Contextualizing Christianity is an effective, biblical way to help people come close to Christ (the apostle Paul was a master of it), and it's not wrong or bad to talk about the gospel in ways that connect with specific contexts and specific groups of people. And as missions-focused activists, many evangelicals were involved in contextualizing the gospel to other cultures too!

But I started to realize that, over time, many of us evangelicals had chosen to go even further. We had begun to mark our personal cultural contextualizations as "what the Bible teaches," effectively enshrining our culture as "the only way to follow Jesus." Which of course closed the door on contextualizing Christianity for other cultures—because we saw our contextualization as the *definition* of Christianity, rather than as merely an expression of it. We started to export our contextualized Christianity rather than contextualizing the gospel within other cultures. All of which is to say that I realized that many people of color who attended my churches or my school had to become fluent in majority culture to belong. No wonder many left evangelicalism for other expressions of Christianity.

As you can imagine, this realization set off more than just discomfort. I found myself in an emotional crisis, a lot of which centered around reexamining spiritual things I'd been taught to make sure they were true, including things like the uniqueness of the Christian faith, the trustworthiness of Scripture, the person of Jesus, justice issues, and more. In many ways, this desire to experience the truth of Christ firsthand rather than being told about it is still cascading through my faith. Instead of learning about what the Bible says solely from "trusted experts," I began exploring God's words directly, listening to the community of faith and the Holy Spirit. My Christian culture in the past told me that we could know all the answers and, having achieved "the right answers," could rest secure in a static faith—but now I know that the life of faith means we should never stop learning and growing.

Some of my discomfort with the evangelical church and the United States is that I am still part of both. I am still an evangelical, still deeply connected in that community, and I identify myself within it. I am still a citizen of the United States. My critiques and problems are not about "them" but about "us." Which means that when I see places where the world is not as it should be in the evangelical church or in the United States, as I work to hopefully bring shalom to them, I have to hold space for my own part in those systems.

How do I manage that discomfort now? I'd say the major thing I'm working on is creating faith spaces that are comfortable for people outside my church traditions. The way I talk and the topics I address in life and on social media have shifted audiences. I'm far more interested in speaking to people outside the traditional church and helping them see Jesus well. Sometimes this means calling out behavior within the church, holding it up and saying loudly, "Just to be clear, this is not Christian behavior." Why? Because this tells my non-Christian friends, "This gross thing you see is not about Jesus." Which means they stay open to Jesus even if they're against this specific church (where they weren't welcome anyway). This has created some conflict with some other Christians, who see me as negative about the church. I'm not actually negative about the church. I love the people of God . . . and we're in this together. We're all citizens of God's Kingdom.

Kathy

Matt, I'm curious what you were taught about or have experienced around conflict. I was taught that conflict, especially in public, was a bad thing. Conflict was supposed to be in whispers in private, though I also learned that whispers can be really loud. In another chapter, you wrote about church conflict and church splits, which also was common for me. For you, was conflict a good or bad thing? Do you have any examples of a conflict being resolved well and resulting in peacemaking? Or will we have to wait until heaven?

Matt

Ironically, I was taught that conflict at its best was incredibly civil. Yes, there was the biblical injunction of going to the one who harmed you, then bringing a friend, et cetera (and again, because of the contextualization of evangelicalism, not mentioning that Scripture talks about multiple ways to deal with conflict, not just this one). But yes, civility and politeness above all. "Pardon me, sir, I'm sure this is unintentional, but I believe you are stabbing me repeatedly in the back." Of course, this doesn't work well in every situation, so gossip and whisper campaigns become a way to deal with issues. Because gossip and whispers are "secret," there is deniability. It's a backchannel way to deal with the failings of our own conflict theories.

I've found that moving others and myself toward honesty does more to remove conflict than anything else. There are too many people who take advantage of civility and secrecy to manipulate. Every time someone says to me, "So-and-so said this bad thing about you," I bring that other person into the loop. Always. I try not to accept anonymous feedback or ever take secondhand critique as something that was actually communicated.

For instance, when I was a missionary, a coworker began going around telling people I had said some things I had not. When I heard about it, I sat down with the person who had told me, then called up the person who was gossiping and put them on speakerphone. As soon as I was on the call, their story changed completely. Our mutual friend had "misunderstood." Every time I heard the rumor, I repeated this process. That coworker got pretty tired of hearing from me.

Can conflict be well resolved and result in peacemaking? Absolutely. A lot of it has to do with our character when we screw up, though. A few summers ago, an older (in his seventies) white man who I really respect was talking to some young (in their twenties) people of color at a conference, and he said a variety of things that were offensive. Now, some of this was generational rather than racial (that is, he was saying things in a way that was misunderstood because of communication differences generationally). And some of the things were truly ignorant about race, ethnicity, and culture.

Here's what happened: The people of color reached out to some other people in the organization—leaders and people they respected. They shared their experience and said, "Are we reading this right? This is problematic, isn't it?" They shared how they were feeling (it wasn't good). Those leaders affirmed them and said they were right to feel that way and set up a meeting with the older leader.

And to his credit, he sat and listened and asked questions. He worked through the misunderstandings and stared without flinching at his own shortcomings. He was truly brokenhearted that he had hurt these folks—and shocked, too, because he had been giving parts of this talk for years and had no idea.

The result was that the young people *loved* him. They went on and on about how wonderful he was. There were lots of hugs and tears, and the relationship deepened rather than fractured. But it required a lot of courage (both to speak up and to listen). But this is shalom: The place of conflict is opportunity for repair. And sometimes that which is repaired is stronger than what was there before.

CHAPTER 5

PATIENCE

The Chapter You've All Been Waiting For

Kathy

I HAVE HEARD SEVERAL YOUTH PASTORS use the story of Jacob and Rachel as an example of patience, especially in the context of marriage and dating. I'll summarize the story: Jacob—grandson of Abraham and son of Isaac—fell in love with a woman named Rachel. Back in biblical times, marriage was a transaction, where the girl or woman was exchanged for something of value—animals, money, labor. Jacob could marry Rachel if he worked seven years for her father, who happened to also be Jacob's uncle. Jacob agreed because, after all, he was in love. On the wedding night, however, he realized he had been married to Leah, Rachel's older sister. In the end, Jacob (who, you should also remember, deceived his father and stole his older brother's blessing and inheritance) was allowed to bring Rachel in as his second wife, with the stipulation that he would work another seven years for his now father-in-law.

The moral of the story goes something like this: Jacob waited for his first love. Jacob worked fourteen years to be married and take his favored wife wherever he wanted. That is patience, so I've been told.

Yes, but also *no*. Set aside for a moment the commodification of women as goods or the fact that Leah and Rachel, literal sister wives in a culturally patriarchal context, had no agency in this decision. While Jacob may not have gotten his first choice after the first seven years, he did get a wife, and he was able to bring Rachel home a week after his wedding to Leah. He got what he wanted, no extra patience required. He just got tricked in the process (non-Christians would call this karma).

Now, this is not a romantic story, and no youth pastor or pastor, period, should use it as an example of how to pursue marriage. But beyond that, this narrative portrays patience as a contract. And yes, that is what biblical marriage is and was—but a contract is not the context for true patience. When one bears patience as the fruit of the Spirit, there is no guaranteed outcome.

Patience in a much broader context is a willingness and ability to sit and endure without acting out, to be long-suffering without complaint, and to refrain from retaliation when provoked. Patience is waiting with no assurance that things will work out the way you want.

That kind of patience, when you have nothing to lose because you have already lost everything, makes me think of the bleeding woman in Luke 8. How we don't know her name. How we only know her by her label as "unclean." She spent twelve years bleeding, twelve years unable to fully participate in community, twelve years spending all her money on doctors and not getting better. When we see her in Scripture, no one is advocating for her or even standing by her. Her patience lasted twelve years, and then she decided enough was enough—and reached out for the hem of Jesus' cloak.

Patience is waiting twelve years for this chance and then holding your breath in fear, hoping Jesus isn't serious when he asks his disciples,

"Who touched me?"[1] Patience is waiting and then discerning it's finally time to say something and tell your story, even when you have no idea how the crowd, the disciples, or Jesus will respond.

Patience is a long, measured steadiness, a practice of intention, of noticing and acting when the time is right. It is deciding how and when to make your point or when to listen and ask questions. It is loving over time that weighs multiple factors—urgency, capacity, trust, possibility of change, and many more. In loving disagreements, patience honors the humanity of every person and holds the tension of how healthy conflict and resolution impacts everyone.

The Slow Work of Patience

The book of Galatians and the story of the bleeding woman were written when traveling was measured in days and weeks, not because of flight cancellations but because people moved at a different pace than we do today, and they faced unpredictable circumstances along the way. The only modern examples I can think of are refugees and asylum seekers traveling to find safety beyond their borders with no guarantees for travel, arrival, or welcome.

Generally, our perception of time—and the patience required to move through it—is different now. We live in an immediate-gratification world and have immediate-gratification expectations. We used to dial phones that were connected to the wall; now we carry phones that operate like small computers in our back pockets. We can find out-of-season fruits and vegetables in a grocery store. Amazon delivers whatever we want in a day or two. Our communication is instantaneous—if I text you, do not leave me on "read" for more than ten minutes.

But patience isn't just about delaying gratification. Patience is about being able to hold in tension the *now* and the *not yet*. Patience is sitting with your child's disappointment at not making the team, knowing that the sting is real and deep in the moment—and also that there will come a time when he will have found his thing. Patience is sitting with suffering—our own or that of another—without solutions.

Our first child was a bit of a surprise. My doctor was surprised I had gotten pregnant because I had lost so much weight during a rather stressful few months at work. When we tried for a second child, though—nothing. Nothing for two years. Then I had surgery for endometriosis and was told to try again. Two lines, and the wait was over.

Until it wasn't. I was at the end of my first trimester, morning/all-day sickness raging, and Peter and I went to my appointment eager to see and hear a heartbeat. We didn't. We could see it immediately in the face of our ultrasound technician, and then our doctor came in right away. A blood test confirmed what we had feared. I had a D and C procedure that week and came home devastated.

In the days following, we learned a lot about how our Christian friends understood the grief of miscarriage and how they felt about our grief. Most attempts at consolation were about moving past the grief—*don't worry; be grateful you already have one child; you can try again because you are so young.* We wanted to be patient and sit in our grief, and we wanted friends and family to do the same. Even then, a slower time with wireless phones and dial-up internet, many people in our community could not sit patiently and hold grief in tension with hope. Instead they wanted, with the best of intentions, to find quick ways to ease our pain . . . and perhaps their own discomfort.

Patience requires an ability to sit with discomfort and sit with others, our own community, and other communities in their suffering. As we learn to hold that with them, we move toward a deeper understanding of someone else's experience, and we can be better friends, family, neighbors, and humans. I started out in campus ministry with an Asian American college fellowship, but my interactions and then relationships with Black ministry staff and students taught me about patience in the midst of disagreement. It wasn't something I said but my presence as an Asian American woman that brought up concerns and emotions for a Black student who had negative interactions specifically with Korean Americans in her hometown. She showed maturity and patience in recognizing her discomfort—which I wrongly interpreted as disinterest and disrespect—and in asking Bob, a Black man and senior staff, to help her and eventually help us. The three of us spent part of the day talking about how our communities misunderstood and hurt one another. That one conversation didn't solve everything, but it helped shift what could've been a different kind of interaction into one of mutuality. This kind of patience is absolutely necessary as we look at the work of repairing communities and relationships. When our lack of patience collides with a real urgency for action in a fast-paced culture, fighting only increases. But patience creates space—not ignoring the urgency or need for change but helping us hold the tensions in our hands so we can take a breath, look at what is happening and what our role is, and discern the next steps forward.

The Different Paths of Patience

How we live out patience doesn't look just one way. My patience with a difficult loved one will show up differently than Matt's patience with a Twitter troll. Patience is a series of different paths, each reflecting a unique situation or emerging from a specific context. When we pause to reflect how patience looks different for the person beside us, we're more equipped to extend patience to others and with ourselves.

One way we can think about patience is in terms of different degrees or levels. No level is necessarily better or more difficult than the other, but I find it helpful to map the movement of patience from our inner life into an outward expression as we engage with others:

- **Pet-peeve patience:** We start in our heart of hearts, the kind of internal patience where we have to count to ten because we can't stand _____ (the sound of someone chewing food, slow drivers in the left passing lane, drivers who don't signal, having to stand behind someone who has not decided on their order at the fast-food restaurant, et cetera). This category usually doesn't involve actual contact with someone, though others around you may experience your reaction.

- **Stranger patience:** This is where you must engage with a stranger in a situation that tests your patience (walking through crowds, encountering slow service at a restaurant, seeing someone try to cut into line ahead of you, et cetera).

- **"Your people" patience:** This is how you respond every morning when only a fraction of the family is ready to leave or when your friend is perpetually late to hangouts. In this circle of relationship, we can either keep a tally or learn to let certain things go and choose to address others.

- **All the things (*waves hands in the air*) patience:** The world is literally burning, every other week there is another mass shooting or incident of excessive force by law enforcement, and annually weather-related disasters reveal failing infrastructure. This is where some of us are waving our hands in the air and screaming, "How are we going to fix any of this?"

Our cultural background and context also inform both our experience and our expression of patience, and we need a level of cultural intelligence as we live and work in multicultural environments. For example, in my Korean American upbringing, patience emphasized long-suffering without complaint. So long as the family or community was doing well, individual complaints had to be withheld. The problem with this model is that if we are all operating this way, how do we know whether anyone is suffering or uncomfortable? Well, we don't. Unless I ask, I might assume that because no one has rocked the boat, the boat is fine. Put that in contrast, for example, with a white American who was raised to understand that the squeaky wheel gets the grease. While I might see her loudly expressing what is bothering her as impatient and demanding, she sees this as a normal and appropriate assertion of her individuality. Each of us becomes better in our interactions when we pursue awareness of and patience with our cultural differences.

Another example of cultural values imposed on our understanding of patience is our concept of time. I love to joke that time, much like race, is a social construct. Being on time is a value in Western culture. In the West, when I am on time, I'm showing respect and honoring my word to the person with whom I have an appointment. But in other cultures, "running late" isn't as significant. The assumption is that something more important held you behind and you were paying attention to that relationship first. If you are running late, your next appointment is expected to be patient and assume you had something more pressing to finish.

Even as we learn different expressions of patience, however, we must recognize that not every expectation of patience is valid. Opposing or conflicting values cannot be considered a matter of opinion when the dignity or safety of another human being is at stake. If we are truly committed to working through conflict, we must learn how to communicate our values even and especially when people have been harmed. We cannot assume we are all on the same page until we have agreed on a communal set of values and expectations. Communal values help us discern when patience serves the whole community versus when patience is expected to serve the comfort of those with more power.

For example, when marginalized communities voice a desire for a change or a demand for justice, they often hear the refrain "be patient." I see this when Black people I learn from bring up reparations for those whose ancestors were enslaved. Black people are told over and over to be patient, to be grateful for how far things have come, to wait for another election cycle, and so on. Sometimes the response is even "Slavery is over. Get over it." And yet we can see the double standard every year when September 11 rolls around and we hear, "Never forget."

Another way the virtue of patience can be weaponized and warped is when it is used to force victims of abuse to stay in dangerous relationships and circumstances. It is never appropriate to tell someone who is a victim of abuse to "be patient" and stay in a dangerous situation or stay silent about the abuse.

Hopefully we can recognize the misuse of the word *patience*—misuse not only by others but also by ourselves—when it is used to avoid discomfort or deflect or, at its worst, silence or oppress. We can recognize this fruit for what it is when we choose to stay in community, even with those we disagree with. Patience, like every other fruit of the Spirit, should lead toward human flourishing, not away from it.

Human relationships are beautifully complex, and we live in a world that does not reward us for taking time to be human. But developing patience is an invitation from God to pause, listen, and learn—and as we do, we find healthier ways through our loving disagreements.

Building the Muscle of Patience

Patience is a practice and discipline that can be nurtured if we give ourselves time and create communal spaces in which to learn. Think of the time we take to build a strong habit or refine a skill. Or think about a common goal or value your community has worked to achieve or foster. That is what we are doing here: not only for our own individual benefit but toward building a spiritual practice of patience with ourselves and with others.

- **Create spaces of silence.** Our external and internal worlds are so often noisy and busy. Our smartphones might be set on silent, but even the slight buzzing of a phone or watch snaps us back into reality. Is a TV or music playing in the background of your home or even your car? Are you constantly listening to something on your headphones as you go from place to place, whether you're running errands or running? To learn to be patient and simply be present, we must allow space to cultivate that. We must intentionally push back against the ways our lives demand our immediate attention.

Worship and church leaders: Do not be afraid of silence between a sermon and a communal response. One of the most powerful practices is to leave a Good Friday service in silence, to sit and leave with the internal discomfort, sadness, and confusion of the Crucifixion. Do not be afraid to preach and teach about questions that have no easy answers and to let people sit in the discomfort of not knowing.

• **Create spaces for waiting.** One of the traditions of the student group I helped lead was to keep a prayer journal. Each group of students who came to pray would list what they had prayed for. Week after week after month after quarter, they would return to the notebook and look at what prayers had been answered and how they had been answered. Sometimes prayers would go unanswered, but had the students not had a physical reminder, many of those prayers would have been forgotten. That written record was a reminder to keep praying, to keep gathering, to keep waiting together.

One of my favorite traditions we added to our family when our kids were little was Advent. The end of the calendar year was full of social activities, school projects, and the general rush toward the holidays. We set aside a few minutes each Sunday evening of Advent to quietly light a candle. It didn't have to be a whole thing, just a few minutes to remind us we were waiting for

Christmas. I've tried incorporating that kind of countdown and stillness in the lead-up to other significant days or even projects.

- **Create space to do the deep work.** I wrote in an earlier chapter that I have anxiety and depression. I am also a recovering perfectionist, and my inner critic is most often the loudest voice I hear. My impatience runs deep because when something does not go perfectly, I can think of at least a dozen things I could have done to prevent it all from going off the rails. My fear of imperfection emerges in its most ugly form when I lash out at the ones I love most. Patience requires knowing what activates our knee-jerk reactions and why we respond the way we do, especially when our behavior is unloving and unkind.

  Parenting young children was incredibly challenging for me. I felt like every day I was enduring, waiting, long-suffering, but too often I retaliated, reacted in frustration, acted out, and complained. One of my worst moments was when I raised an open hand and slapped one of my children across the face. I was more than just impatient—I let my frustration take over. And instead of being a loving, patient mother, I slapped my child. I apologized profusely, cried, and maybe still beat myself up over this mistake.

  What followed were years of a combination of therapy, medication, and spiritual direction to help me do the deep work of understanding and recognizing how and why anger and frustration manifested the way it did in my soul and body. I needed to recognize my own woundedness and how I saw similar situations dealt with growing up. Professionals helped me recognize ways in which I had absorbed and mirrored unhealthy patterns of communication, and they guided me into new and better ways to communicate and release my anger and pain.

• **Create space for rest.** Even practicing patience cannot be done twenty-four seven. Too often rest is seen and commodified as a privilege, but the reality is that we are all created for and need rest.

Resting means not only going to bed at a reasonable hour and disconnecting from our electronic gadgets but also finding ways as the body of Christ to give one another a chance to rest. If longer forms of rest seem inaccessible, look within your community to see who has resources that can be shared, such as babysitting, an extra car, or points for a night at a hotel. For many years, our family couldn't afford "real" vacations, so we planned our road trips around friends who opened their homes. When a friend of mine was sleep-deprived while her husband was on a business trip, I had her come over so she could sleep while Peter and I held her baby. (That's when our kids decided they didn't want another sibling.)

Church leaders, make sure your pastoral team takes a sabbatical free from the responsibilities of weekly sermons and congregational visits. Budget time and money so that your pastors can get away with their families (and maybe a few days without) and just play. Church leaders, you, too, will burn out, so don't keep people on for extra terms. If you can't find volunteers, maybe you need to look at what you're asking people to do.

Patience, like all the fruit of the Spirit, is a reminder that we do not enter the Christian life alone. It's an invitation into the body of Christ where we depend on one another for the health and flourishing of the whole. Remember, living more out of the fruit of the Spirit doesn't just change you or me individually. When I grow in patience, I am able to listen and wait for others, allowing them the freedom to respond, knowing we are creating a space of mutual respect. Instead of fostering an environment that demands a specific type of response, patience roots itself in love and leaves room for trust, growth, and change.

Matt

Oof. Kathy's definition of patience (and examples throughout the chapter) really zeroed in on something in my own life. She said patience is both "a willingness and ability to sit and endure without acting out" and that it involves "refrain[ing] from retaliation when provoked."

I couldn't help but notice that the opposite of this is not so much impatience as it is anger. The times I'm most likely to struggle with patience are when I'm mad. We use a lot of other words to disguise our anger: *impatience, frustration, annoyance*. A lot of times, these are just nicer ways of saying *furious*. I love that Kathy's suggestions for building patience are the same kinds of things that work for defusing anger. Creating spaces for silence and rest, waiting, and doing deep work in our souls.

For myself, though, I'm going to need to sit with that "refrain[ing] from retaliation when provoked" for a while. A work friend and I made a pact that we would never respond to an email while angry. We realized that both of us made more work for ourselves when we sent a note to our coworkers while angry—sometimes because we were unclear and sometimes because we were, um, maybe a little too clear.

I remember so clearly a day she called me when I was still driving to work, about twenty minutes away, and she was furious. "I've written a scathing email," she said, "and I'm about to hit send, but I'm calling so you have a chance to tell me not to do it. But I really want to."

I told her, "Well, I'm only twenty minutes away, and then we can look at it together." (I didn't tell her that the email she was responding to was making me angry too!) I got to work and she had calmed down a bit, and I had calmed down a bit, and we decided to try to calm ourselves before sending the email. So we took a day and responded the next morning.

So many times when there's an argument in the family of faith, we could have more productive disagreement if we just took a day, a week, maybe a month to cool off before continuing the conversation. I'm going to need to think on that for a while.

Kathy, one thing I respect so much about you is how transparent and vulnerable you are with your own life. You're so generous with your own story. Can you share a little more about the healing process after slapping your kid (for you and them)? I imagine that has taken some serious patience.

Kathy

So that child does not remember this happening. I've asked. I am hoping that it isn't a repressed memory, but we also have lots of conversations about therapy. The hardest part was forgiving myself. I've mentioned that my inner critic is very loud, and for years that slap reverberated in my body whenever I felt impatient and angry. I would replay that incident in my mind, even when I had kept a calm voice and handled a situation well. It was like I was still punishing myself. Obviously I still remember the incident, but over time I've learned that it or any other mistake does not define who I am, doesn't determine how I will respond in the present or future, and isn't going to change how God sees me. It's taken time, self-reflection, and professional help. That experience (and my work around it) also reminds me to not define anyone else by a single incident or disagreement.

Matt

Sometimes patience in relationships can be remembering that the person we're in relationship with is still learning and growing (and so, hopefully, are we). What do you do when someone is growing too slowly for your own personal preference (asking for a friend, ha ha)?

Kathy

I have a lot more patience for my children, who are all in their twenties, than I do for just about anyone else. Truly.

I am probably the most impatient with Peter, my husband of thirty years. You'd think I'd have learned to be more patient with him by now, but maybe I am still taking my time because I assume we have at least a lifetime to figure it out.

Almost twenty years ago, I was in a conflict with our pastor. Peter and I were both leaders—I was the worship director and Peter was the treasurer. I had some very strong feelings about what was happening and why, and what I thought was going to happen—and because I am who I am, I wanted to leave the church. Peter is not quite as confrontational as I am, and he would fully admit now that his tendency to avoid conflict and his denial of the cultural misogyny and patriarchy we were experiencing in the church are why he didn't want to leave.

It's a variation of most conflicts, isn't it? One person sees it one way; the other person sees it another way. Both people want to handle the situation differently. You can choose to each handle it the way you want.

I did a lot of unhealthy yelling at Peter, which I've apologized for because, as frustrated as I was with him not wanting to leave the church, he wasn't the core of the church conflict. This is when I/you/we have to decide: *How do you protect yourself from harm?* and *How do you support the other person in their learning and growth?* The answers will look different for each of us, but those were the questions I asked myself and operated out of as I waited for Peter to figure out what I was seeing and experiencing. I stepped out of leadership and removed myself from unnecessary situations with the pastor. I stopped yelling at Peter and found better ways of communicating my concerns to him about our church situation. It took a few months. I continued to go to church, but I was emotionally and spiritually checked out. As I chose patience over anger, though, Peter eventually saw what was happening and we left the church together.

Sometimes, Matt, the other person doesn't learn or grow at our preferred pace, and we have to decide if the relationship can remain healthy even if we disagree. There have been times where I have not spoken to someone for months. Some of those relationships have been repaired because we came together to talk things out over time. Some of those relationships just could not be repaired.

The advent of social media and parasocial relationships has also changed the ways we communicate, for better and for worse. The internet has opened up ways of connecting that some of us could never have imagined, and sometimes we may find ourselves in a virtual friendship or have a virtual acquaintance who starts to interact in a way we did not expect. What then? We have to decide how much energy and actual influence we have with that person. Can we help that person learn? Will they receive our feedback as caring and engage in honest exchanges offline and online? If all your communications with that person are via a social-media platform, do you want to engage publicly online or face-to-face? Are you okay using the "block" or "unfriend" option? There are no easy answers, but having patience with the other person doesn't always mean a relationship will deepen or even continue.

CHAPTER 6

KIND OF A BIG DEAL

Embracing Kindness in a Cruel World

Matt

ONCE UPON A TIME, I WROTE ONLINE that "we should show kindness to others, even when we disagree about important things like abortion." Among the responses I discovered an angry group of people who mocked the idea that kindness was good. I was writing about a painful, difficult topic, so I figured emotions were running high. But there was something particularly strange about these people: They all claimed to be followers of Jesus.

One commenter said, "Kindness isn't a Christian virtue, it's a Hallmark greeting card." I was surprised by this one. When the word *kindness* appears in the New Testament, it's often in "virtue lists." The passage about the fruit of the Spirit is one of those places where the Bible lists a whole "bunch" (pun intended) of virtues and says, "This is what it looks like if you've got the Holy Spirit planted in your life." Kindness is, by any reasonable definition I can think of, a Christian virtue.

I looked at this guy's online presence, and to call him "unkind" would be fair. There was a lot of bullying, name-calling, and aggressive comments. I started pushing into his opinion further, honestly seeking understanding. I asked, "What made you say this? Why did you think kindness is un-Christian? Where was this coming from?"

He explained it like this: "Christians must be truth speakers. The truth is not always kind, and the truth is the most important thing. So if the truth is cruel, then we must be cruel."

Now, this guy was wrong. Spectacularly, incredibly wrong. But I couldn't stop thinking about it. If this guy, who said he was a follower of Jesus, thought that kindness got in the way of following Jesus, what did that mean? And how on earth did he come to that conclusion?

As I talked more with him, I realized that his definition of kindness was "being nice." Which, again, is the same sort of reason that Kathy and I didn't want to write a book about civility. Christians are called to something much larger and more difficult than being nice, and something more complicated and harder to achieve than civility.

I couldn't stop thinking about his statement: "Kindness isn't a Christian virtue, it's a Hallmark greeting card." If we've decided that kindness is best relegated to superficial niceness and disposable good wishes, then we've probably gotten far from what being kind actually means for someone with a heavenly passport.

I wanted to see what the Scripture really says about it, and what followed might be the most interesting and fun word study I've ever done. We're going to take a deep dive into this word and then get to the practical part: what it looks like to incorporate kindness into our lives. So get ready for a chapter about language, puns, medieval knights, and what it means to be a follower of Jesus, the Kind One.

The Greek Word for Kindness

A while back, there was a popular phrase that would get tossed around from time to time: "Netflix and chill." What this little slang phrase meant to the generation using it was "Do you want to come to my place and watch something we can ignore and have sex?" Meanwhile, for people another generation or two up, the word *chill* definitely just meant "hang out."

You probably know where this is going.

I had some friends in college ministry—Gen Xers—who sent a note to all their college students inviting them over to "Netflix and chill." There was deep horror among the students. As someone in my generation might have said, "You keep using that word. I do not think it means what you think it means."[1] Once it was all explained to the ministers, they sent a horrified apology and a clarification that they were inviting students to (how do you say it?) "hang out and watch movies."

When we start talking about "what a word meant in Greek," we run into a similar problem. Translators do their best to find words that are roughly the same in both languages, but there are so many ways that can fail. Slang, meanings of words shifting, or just the fact that sometimes there's no direct translation. Languages don't always have a word that means exactly the same thing as a word in another language. Some words have multiple possible meanings in one language, and a word that is a wonderful fit for one meaning might be a terrible fit in another context.

This is true of the Greek word χρηστός. (We'll copy it over as *chrēstos*.) This is the word we translate as "kind" or sometimes "good" and even as "morals." And that's because, actually, this word can mean any of those things depending on how it's used in Greek. The word is rooted in the idea along these lines: something that's a good fit, something useful. But it can also mean easy, good, gracious, kind, or pleasant.[2]

This word most often appears in the Bible with phrases like "be kind to each other" or "God is kind" or virtue lists where *kindness* comes along with *faithfulness* and *gentleness* and so on. The writers of Scripture assume that we sort of know what kindness is already. There's not much context to tell us what the word means.

So I started digging around in ancient Greek texts outside the Bible to see if I could find a few examples where someone explained the word or at least gave examples of what kindness looks like. There were some fun ones—for example, the Greeks would sometimes describe wine as *chrēstos*. Maybe they meant that it was useful, exactly what they needed at that moment. Or maybe they were just expressing that it was good.

Chrēstos was also a common name for Greek slaves—the idea being that this was a person who was useful to their master. If you're like me, you have complicated feelings about slavery in the ancient world and how it's talked about in Scripture. But the point is that this was a name given to slaves who were doing a good job, the ones you could count on to do what was needed.

And maybe the most helpful was old Aristotle, who couldn't help but define everything he talked about. The apostle Paul, who wrote Galatians and our passage about the fruit of the Spirit, was well versed in his Greek philosophers, so whether Aristotle's definition is exactly what Paul meant or not, it's something he would have been aware of. Aristotle said that kindness is "helpfulness towards someone in need, not in return for anything, nor for the advantage of the helper himself, but for that of the person helped."[3]

Notice that in these different Greek usages—whether a bottle of wine, the slave, or Aristotle's definition—meeting someone's needs is a central piece. It's not about being polite (how we sometimes think of kindness). It's not a "Hallmark greeting card." It's something more than well wishes or being gentle with our words. Kindness is active. A kind person sees what is needed and then provides it.

The Knights of Kindness

So how do we take this really rich Greek word, *chrēstos*, and translate it? We've already talked about how it means someone who is useful, someone who is actively looking for problems and fixing them. Someone who's helpful toward people in need with no thought of reward, no desire for payment. English doesn't have a word that means all those things.

Early Bible translations tried a bunch of different words: *goodness*, *gentleness*, even *benignity* (looking at you, Mr. Wycliffe). These are all words that make sense and capture some aspect of what *chrēstos* is. Kindness and goodness in particular are so close that they were sometimes interchangeable, depending on the context.

While I don't know for sure whether it was the first Bible to adopt the word *kindness* in Galatians, the English Revised Version used it in the nineteenth century. This was a revision of the King James Bible, and the translators decided that *kindness* was the right word. Since then, it has become the go-to translation for many modern editions of the Bible.

And I love this word, for a variety of reasons.

In English, the word *kindness* goes back to the Old English word *kyndnes*, which meant, roughly, "nation." But the idea of it came from one's family (kin) and relations. *Kindness* was about your nation, your people, and the feelings you had about them. It's a word about the fierce loyalty some of us have for our own families—and the generosity and care we give them as a result.

Think of it like this: In a healthy family, you're going to try to help your "kin" if they have a need, right? If I'm driving to work and I see a stranger whose car is broken down on the side of the road, I might not stop. But if it's my sister or my cousin or my kid, I'll stop for sure, even if I'm going to be late for work.

When I stop to help a stranger in need, I'm treating them like my kin. I'm showing them kindness. Kindness is seeing a need and doing active good for other people, just like you would for your family.

But the word got even better as it continued to grow over the centuries. As *kyndnes* slowly became *kindness*, the meaning of the word expanded too. As it came into Middle English, *kindness* grew and changed to mean, roughly, "courtesy, noble deeds."[4] This happened during the Middle Ages, around the fourteenth century.

So imagine, if you will, knights setting out from King Arthur's Round Table, looking for good deeds to be done. They did this for the sake of their nation, to honor God and the king. They eagerly went out looking for something kind they could do for others. They were seeking people in trouble, people they could help in some way.

The English word *kindness* really began to take on exactly the meaning that Aristotle encouraged: actively seeking to provide for the needs of others.

A Punny Thing Happened on the Way to the Forum

Now let's backtrack in time a little bit to a delightful linguistic misunderstanding. I hope you'll enjoy it as much as I did.

So in Greek we have the word for "kind" (χρηστός), and then we have a really similar word that's going to cause some trouble. The word is χριστός. As you might notice, there's just one little letter difference: an ι instead of η. And, even worse, the two words sound almost identical when they're said out loud. The first word we already know: it's *chrēstos*, and we often translate it as "kind." The second word is *Christos*, which means "anointed one," and we translate it as "Christ."[5]

A Greek speaker hearing these words might not have been able to tell the difference between Jesus the Kind One and Jesus the Christ. And, in fact, it appears that this misunderstanding was common. We have a variety of ancient documents that misspelled *Christ* as *Chrest* . . . and even *Christian* as *Chrestian*. There were people out there in the early days of the church who definitely thought that Jesus' name was Jesus Chrēstos. It's a big difference. Some people heard a common slave name that meant "useful and kind." Some people heard "anointed one," which meant, *This guy has been chosen by God to be a prophet or to be king, maybe both*.

We even have some copies of the Scriptures that contain the misspelling, including a pretty famous one called Codex Sinaiticus, one of the earliest and most complete Greek Bibles. What's extra hilarious in Sinaiticus is that the word is misspelled *Chrestian* and then someone corrected the misspelling to *Christian*. So we have a pun,[6] a typo, and a correction. Pretty fun!

So look, this doesn't mean that there was some other guy named Jesus Chrēstos or that the Bible isn't true because people wrote the name down wrong. This is just a side effect of living in a culture where plenty of people were illiterate, multiple languages were spoken, and word of mouth was often how news got around.

What I love about this little linguistic quirk, though, is that it tells us something about the early followers of Jesus. To the people who knew and interacted with them, it made perfect sense that these followers of Jesus had a God called "Jesus the Kind One." And calling those followers "little kind ones" (Chrestians) made sense too. Jesus was kind, and his early followers were also kind. They had the Holy Spirit, after all, and part of the fruit of the Spirit is kindness.

The Kindness of Christ

That early confusion about *Christians* and *Chrestians* makes me wonder how easily people today might mistake "those really kind people" in a conversation for "the Christians." But that's what it looks like to be citizens of heaven: our citizenship should be apparent, even remarkable to people around us. When we're equipped and empowered by the Spirit to bear that fruit in our relationships and communities, people should take notice. So how do we get there? Let's dig a little deeper into what the Bible says about how God is *chrēstos*, as well as how people who have the Holy Spirit become *chrēstos*.

Luke tells us that Jesus said, "Love your enemies, do good to them, and lend to them without expecting to get anything back. Then your reward will be great, and you will be children of the Most High, because he is kind [*chrēstos*] to the ungrateful and wicked."[7] This one is fascinating because it so closely matches Aristotle's description of kindness. When Jesus says we'll be children of the Most High, he's saying we'll look like God—just like a lot of kids look like their biological parents. And how does God look? God's the sort of person who loves enemies, does good things, and gives with no expectation of a payback. You know, someone whose "helpfulness towards someone in need, not in return for anything" is evident. God is kind.

When we're in disagreements, it's easy to assume the other party is evil or at least ill-intentioned. Once upon a time, when I was a youth worker at a church college group, this one mom was constantly furious at the staff and saying mean things about the group (her kids loved the group, so it was really weird—we could never figure out what her deal was). She had a meeting with the youth pastor, who started out by asking her, "Are you okay? You seem like you're in a lot of pain." And what had been supposed to be an airing of grievances became a healing moment for this woman as she shared some hurts she had received. The youth pastor showed love to her, expressed kindness, and as a result this "enemy" even became his friend.

Ephesians 4:32 tells us that instead of having malice (an intention to do harm to those we dislike) toward others, we should be *chrēstos* to each other (have an intention to do good to others! You know, kindness!). And I love 1 Peter 2:3, which encourages us to remember that we have "tasted the kindness [*chrēstos*] of the Lord"!

This is one I need to remember a lot when I'm online. It's so tempting in an argument to get a zinger in (I'm pretty good at zingers!) and show how foolish or wrong the other person is. But that so often does harm to the other person rather than good. I try to remember that the short-term win of the stunning comeback doesn't mean much if I'm harming someone to make it.

There are a few other places *chrēstos* appears in the New Testament,[8] but my favorite is in Romans 2:4, which tells us that God's *chrēstos* leads us to repentance. God's *kindness* leads us to repentance. Not angry sermons. Not cruel social-media posts. Not "truth even if it hurts your feelings!" God's kindness.

And what we know about kindness makes this verse so beautiful to me.

If kindness is actively seeking the good of others, if kindness is knowing the exact thing that someone needs and then providing it, then when we say "God's kindness leads us to repentance," what we mean is this: God knows us perfectly. God sees exactly what we need to come to an awareness of our broken places and knows how to guide us to a place where we desire God more than those broken things. And God gives us exactly what we need to move into deeper relationship with God and with one another. That's God's kindness bringing us to repentance. How beautiful!

I mean, how beautiful when God does it for me. Knowing that this same kindness is God's expectation of those who live in the heavenly Kingdom is a bit more challenging. But it means that when I am in a disagreement, an argument, a fight with someone, I need to consider this: *How can I do good to this person? What are their deepest needs, and can I help meet them?* In other words, how do I shift my goal in this conversation away from "winning" and toward "doing good for others"? That's a lot to ask! But that's also what it looks like when the Spirit's kindness is growing in our lives.

Radical Kindness

Kindness can be something as small as a well-timed note of encouragement, a quiet word, a little, unasked-for favor. It could be giving someone a ride, sitting with a friend at the doctor's office, mowing your neighbor's lawn when they're out of town. It can be this huge variety of things because it's all about noticing the needs of the people around you, and there's a huge variety of needs in the world.

But kindness is not always easy or superficial. Kindness can require sacrifice, even if it's just of time and attention—and often of much more than that. The action of kindness means seeing the needs of another and moving toward them. It means showing up and following through.

Something that gets lost, I think, in the way we've diminished kindness, the way we've sidelined it as niceness and well-intended feelings, is that the kindness the Holy Spirit can grow within us is powerful. And that Spirit-empowered kindness has the potential to bring about enormous, lasting change in the world.

On January 1, 1900, a man named 杉原千畝 (Chiune Sugihara) was born in Japan. When he got to university, he decided he wanted to be an ambassador. While working as a diplomat in China, Sugihara started attending a Russian Orthodox church to practice his Russian. It was there that he converted to Christianity and became a true follower of Jesus. This changed things in his life and in his career.

As a follower of Jesus the Kind One, Sugihara became a bit of a troublemaker. When he was the Deputy Foreign Minister in Manchuria, he wrote to his superiors that Japanese soldiers were badly mistreating Chinese locals. When nothing changed, he resigned in protest. This decision caused him to lose the posting he had been working toward for years: the embassy in Moscow.

The Japanese government decided instead to put Sugihara somewhere he couldn't make much trouble: Kaunas, Lithuania. It would be a "one man" consulate, requiring no heavy ambassadorial work. What they mostly wanted him to do was keep tabs on the Germans and the Russians and report back home. World War II was starting in earnest.

But Sugihara saw the changes happening in Lithuania. Refugees from all over Europe came to his embassy gates—mostly Jewish people from Poland, fleeing the Nazis. They couldn't get visas, and they begged Sugihara for help.

He couldn't stop thinking about these people. They were in grave danger, and if the Nazis came to Lithuania—which seemed increasingly likely—Sugihara knew how their stories would end. But Japan was Germany's ally. How could he do anything to help?

Sugihara wrote to Japan and asked his superiors for permission to grant these refugees Japanese transit visas. His superiors told him no.

Still, Jewish refugees stood around the consulate walls day and night, exhausted, their clothes torn, their children with them. At first it was only two hundred or three hundred people, but the number kept growing.

Sugihara wrote his superiors again, and again they said, "Do not issue visas." He waited two days, wrote a third time, and received the same answer.

Sugihara's wife, Yukiko, couldn't sleep, and neither could Sugihara. They knew if he disobeyed, he would lose his job. And if the Nazis knew they had helped the Jews, worse could happen. Sugihara and Yukiko had their children to think about too.

But—"I could not allow these people to die," Sugihara later explained. "People who had come to me for help with death staring them in the eyes. Whatever punishment may be imposed upon me, I knew I had to follow my conscience."⁹ He talked about it with Yukiko, and she agreed.

The next day, he started writing visas.

For the next several weeks, he wrote visas for eighteen to twenty hours a day. Yukiko would bring him food and beg him to eat, then she massaged his cramped hands before he would turn to writing again.

The Japanese government ordered Sugihara to stop. He ignored them. Other Japanese citizens were being evacuated, and other consulates were closing down, but not Sugihara's. He refused to leave.

Eventually soldiers arrived to escort Sugihara out of the country. He continued to write visas. At the train station, he continued to write visas, handing them into the crowd. He handed the last one out the carriage window. He bowed to the people as the train departed and said, "Please forgive me. I cannot write anymore. I wish you the best."

We're not sure how many visas Sugihara wrote, but it was at least two thousand. It may have been as many as six thousand. What we do know is that he saved thousands and thousands of lives. Families, neighbors, refugees. An entire Jewish seminary got visas because of Sugihara, the only whole seminary to be spared from the Nazis.

Sugihara did lose his job eventually. He was told it was because of "that situation in Lithuania." He became a traveling salesman in Japan, and most people didn't know his story until many years later, when the people of Israel asked him to come to Israel so they could celebrate what he had done.

According to the Simon Wiesenthal Center, Sugihara's act of kindness saved at least ten thousand people—and those ten thousand survivors have more than forty thousand descendants today.[10]

This is the power of kindness in the world. Sugihara saw a need and took action to meet it.

Kindness is not being nice. It's not a Hallmark card. And in the big question of what to do when we're in conflict and disagreement with one another, kindness is so much more than just putting on a smile and pretending everything is okay. When we are kind, we choose to legitimately seek the best for one another despite the places where we disagree.

Kindness is how we speak to each other. (*Am I doing harm or good toward others?*)

Kindness is how we care for others. (*How can I help this person?*)

Kindness is how we vote. (*What will be the impact of this policy on those around me?*)

Kindness is how we spend our money. (*Where is this money going? What is the impact of that? Am I doing harm or good to the world?*)

As Scripture teaches us, it's God's kindness—not cruelty, not meanness, not malice—that leads us to repentance. And as we become more like God—as we grow in kindness—this must surely have an impact on our relationships in those moments when we have disagreements.

Kindness isn't about being good. It's about doing good.

Kathy

Okay, I am a Gen Xer and *I know what Netflix and chill means.* (And how can you be in college ministry and not know that's what it means?)

My Dear Readers, when Matt and I were assigning chapters, I knew Matt had to write on kindness because between our four podcasting cohosts, Matt is consistently voted the kindest of the bunch. He has a pastoral heart. You can't manufacture that, which is why I want to know, Matt—can speaking truth be kind *and* uncomfortable?

Matt

Ha! The answer is yes. I think one of the reasons people experience me as kind is that I'm always pretty tuned in to those around me. If we're in a group of six, I'm thinking about each person: *What are they thinking? How are they feeling? Why haven't they said anything in a while?* Which is just to say, I'm trying to make sure that what I say and do is understandable to them and includes them. Can speaking truth be both kind and uncomfortable? Absolutely. I tend to make closest friends with people who are completely honest with me (sometimes to the point of rudeness). I like knowing where I stand, and I enjoy that I often see certain things about myself more clearly because of their honesty. I don't think of those friends as unkind, because they love me deeply and don't say those things to harm me—they say them to help.

Where I see our discourse running off the rails sometimes is that we want to bring the truth in the absence of a desire to help the people we're correcting. I know, that's so tricky and getting to that emotional space can be hard (sometimes I'm not the best person to help, and I have to tag out). And I'll be honest: There are people who I've tried to help with kindness or even niceness and they just couldn't hear what I was saying until I laid it out with stark, clear, straightforward words that hurt. But the goal in that situation is to hurt someone just like resetting a bone hurts. If my words aren't designed to heal, why am I in the conversation?

Kathy

You and I both used to be in vocational ministry and relied on the kindness of others to provide financially for our salaries. During my two decades in ministry, I had many churches and donors decide to stop giving. Sometimes it was because financial circumstances had changed, but sometimes it was because they didn't like what they saw happening in my prayer letters or on my social media. Several white colleagues who had never had those types of donor interactions were devastated when donors pulled financial support because the ministry platformed a Black pastor and activist and the worship team wore shirts that said "Black Lives Matter." I remember feeling like the financial support was very much conditional, and historically staff of color were most impacted by these types of "strings." It still doesn't feel very kind to me, and again the responsibility of any conversation and potential repair of the relationship landed on staff of color. Personally, I got tired and stopped trying to repair those relationships. Did you experience any of this? What would a kind reaction be?

Matt

I absolutely experienced this. Being a missionary means being constantly reminded of the best, most generous things about the Christian community—and the worst, most upsetting parts of it too. I lost a lot of supporters over the years (as you say, some of that is normal), and plenty of times it was because they disagreed with something I said or did. Again, that's their prerogative, but it often felt like a power play: Do what I want because I donate to you. It doesn't feel like "giving" at that point. I even lost a few supporters because *other missionaries* reached out to them and "shared concerns" about my support of racial justice.

What would be a kind response? Well, I'll be honest: When someone stopped supporting us, it was often really hurtful and sometimes delivered with unkind words. Which was unfortunate, given the previous generosity. So the kindest thing I could do sometimes was to deal with my own hurt and not allow myself to respond by hurting them back.

Kathy

Kindness is often connected with niceness. Earlier, in your chapter on peace, I wrote a little bit about tone policing and how Christians use tone policing to manage the reactions of others. This happens quite a bit to women and people of color. There are stereotypes around angry Black women, overly emotional Latinas, and shrewd Asian women. As a writer and activist, I'm often told in so many words to be nicer—"You catch more flies with honey than vinegar."

I get tired of that critique because I'm not out to catch flies. Sometimes I intend to burn bridges because they were built with gates and tollbooths to keep me and others on one side of the bridge. I feel a sense of urgency to point out the injustice and to rally others into awareness and action, and that doesn't always lend itself in the moment to language or behavior that is nice. So I am constantly asking myself, *What is the difference between the "niceness" that makes other people comfortable and the kindness that still allows for clear action?* Any thoughts on this, Matt?

Matt

Look, there's a reason that one of the words most often used in defining "nice" is *agreeable*. When we're sitting around trying to decide on a place to eat and I have a slight preference for tacos (okay, maybe a large preference) and you want to get pizza, and I say, "You know what, let's get pizza!"—that's nice. I'm being agreeable. I'm a "go with the flow" kind of guy. You want to go to the later movie? Let's do it. You want me to get up early and help with yardwork? Sure.

Here's the thing, though. You can't be "agreeable" toward injustice. I mean, you can be, and people often are, but you shouldn't be. Let's say I'm in a meeting and someone (accidentally and with no conscious ill intent) says something problematic. Something racist, even, or bigoted in some way, that hurts the feelings of people in the room. I think for a lot of folks the "nice" response would be to (a) let it slide (no harm was intended!) or (b) talk to that person in private. There are situations when that might be appropriate. Is it kind, though? Well, I'd say that if one of my family members was being harmed by what someone was saying in a meeting I would definitely speak up in the moment—because "being nice" to the person doing harm, even if they're doing it unintentionally, can compound the harm. Or, sure, I might tell my family, "I'll take care of this" and do so privately. Could be. But I don't let things that harm my family slide. (Also, conversely, my family is pretty quick to point out when we are causing harm to one another. So speaking up, although embarrassing, can be a gift to people who are harming others accidentally.)

We can always be kind. We needn't always be nice.

CHAPTER 7

GOODNESS

God Is Good All the Time. All the Time, God Is Good.

Matt

I DECIDED TO DO a forty-day fast.

It was kind of a thing in the organization I was part of at the time. Our founder did them annually, and many of the other employees at least tried it out. I was one of the "try it out" people.

Oh, I hated it.

I love food, for one thing. And I love hanging out with people (it's amazing how much of our hang-out time is around some sort of meal or snack or delicious drink). So not only was there no food, but it also made hang-out times weird when people asked, "Are you sure you don't want a bite of these incredibly delicious nachos?"

Other people who had done extended fasts told me that they had rich spiritual experiences during their fasts. I didn't. Like, at all. My spiritual experience was trending downward. I was not having fun.

I was not hearing from God. The whole experience was making me cranky.

When you're doing an extended fast, there are some predictable physical results. You're hungry for a good part of it (at the beginning, anyway—this tapers off). I was cold all the time. I got light-headed if I stood up too fast. Energy levels drop, and having some trouble sleeping is common.

What all this added up to was, for me, having a short temper and becoming easily annoyed. As I watched my own interactions, I'd catch myself thinking, *Whoa, that was an unnecessary response. That wasn't like me.*

"That wasn't like me" is a saying common enough that it should be considered an American idiom. It's usually used as a sort of apology or in conjunction with an apology. It's when we discover that we've hurt someone in words or actions and then say, "I'm sorry. That wasn't like me."

But why would I say, "That wasn't like me"? It actually *was* me. It was exactly like me because it's what I did or said. Every time I catch myself saying this, every time I hear someone else say it, it's a flashing neon sign that tells me that this person sees themself as someone different from who they actually are.

Which, in the end, was the best thing about that fast for me. I realized that I was one person when I was happy and well-fed, and I was someone else when I skipped a few meals. But that brought up a disconcerting question: Which one was the *real* me?

Evil or . . .

I grew up in a Christian tradition that emphasized verses like Jeremiah 17:9 (KJV): "The heart is deceitful above all things, and desperately wicked: who can know it?" The idea being that the deepest desires of your heart were "only evil continually." Human beings were conceived and born in sin.[1]

You could do all the right things, follow all the rules, be a "good person" outwardly, and still be—at the core—a sinful, corrupt, depraved human being. This extended even to babies. Were little children sinful, broken, evil? Absolutely. "There is no one righteous, not even one."[2] I vividly remember being pretty concerned that babies were going to hell if they died, which is when an adult explained "the age of account-ability" to me (insert no scriptural references, as this was a purely philo-sophical construct). The basic idea of "age of accountability" was: "It's pretty awful to imagine God sending dead babies to hell, so we have to assume that even though they were sinful, they were too innocent even to understand salvation and therefore God probably sort of grandfathers them in." But the "age of accountability" wasn't available to adults, even if they were part of some remote tribe who had never heard the gospel.

It was all a little vague. What was clear was this: You're evil. I'm evil. Our hearts are broken, maybe beyond repair. The thoughts and desires in our lives are to be distrusted, fought against, resisted, and brought under control.

Because at the end of the day, evil isn't (just) something we do. It's who we are.

What this eventually translated to was the idea that what I most deeply wanted to do was by definition evil, and if God was asking me for something in my life, it would almost always be (again, by defini-tion) something I didn't want to do or give. If I wanted to be a dentist, God almost certainly wanted me to be a missionary. If I wanted to be a missionary, I needed to check myself for evil motivations related to that. I had to be careful not to love my girlfriend too much, or she would become an idol.

This also meant that one of the best ways to control the core evil of teenaged Christian kids like myself was through really strict rules designed to protect us from ourselves and one another. So instead of a "no gambling" rule, we weren't allowed any sort of playing cards on campus. There were no dances allowed because it would almost certainly lead to sex (in fact, the antidancing vibe was so strong that a common joke in these circles is "No sex allowed; that might lead to dancing").

Everywhere I turned, I was told that my core self was soaked in evil; it was so depraved that I couldn't trust my own instincts, desires, or thoughts. But the goodness that comes from life in the Spirit is the shocking opposite of that whole idea.

...Good

Goodness is when our hearts become transformed, when our deepest self is the opposite of "only evil continually." Transformed by the Spirit, our hearts become consumed with the desire to do good, to be kind, to protect others, to love and care for people. Goodness is not something we do; it is someone we become. Though our goodness eventually shows up in our actions, our actions aren't what make us good.

Because goodness isn't an action but a state of being, it's hard to describe or define it. But I know it when I see it. I know it when I feel it. I know it when I experience it in others.

There are a variety of things I've done wrong in my life—some of which still cause me enormous regret or shame—but there are also times when I've done something righteous or beautiful or wonderful. Not because I overcame selfishness or something like that, but because it was something I deeply desired to do, something I wanted to do.

People will sometimes say, "You never know what you will do in a crisis," meaning those situations reveal something about your character. Goodness, I think, tends to show up most clearly under pressure, when we just react and don't have time to plan or think through how we want to be.

Years ago my wife and I saw some kids beating up a third kid on the side of the road. I left my wife in the car, ran through traffic, and chased the bullies off. As my wife pointed out later, that wasn't smart or wise, but I would argue it was still good. Protecting a harmless child who was curled up on the ground while getting kicked . . . that has to be a good thing, I think.

When we instinctively react toward good—when it overflows from a hidden and unconscious place—that's not about hard work.

It's not about fighting our sin nature.

It's about letting the Spirit work in us to change and transform us so that our deepest self desires the same things God does.

When I first learned that human beings can be good, it was such a radical departure from what I had been taught that I found it, frankly, unbelievable. I had always found arguments about "whether humans are basically good or bad" ridiculous. Of course humans are basically bad. The earliest I remember scoffing at this question was when I was quite young, reading a *World's Finest* comic book in which Batman and Superman had an argument about whether human beings were, at the core, basically good or evil.[3] I always preferred Superman, but I had to admit Batman had the better argument (of course, his parents were killed in front of him when he was a kid, so maybe his position was an obvious one to take).

But how can this be? Can human beings become good? Can we truly be creatures who, at our deepest core, are good rather than evil? I believe Scripture is very clear on this. But we have to start with where this goodness comes from, with what moves and animates and transforms us into people who are good and do good. We have to remind ourselves what Scripture says about a good God.

God Is So Good

Scripture is really clear that God is good—full stop, no further conversation needed. But sometimes life can be so painful, or God can seem so silent or distant or even involved in our pain, that we may find ourselves asking if God's actually so good. Friend, if you're in a moment like that, if you're not feeling it or seeing it now, I know that's a hard place to be. So even if you are there right now, let me say this, even if it's hard to believe in this moment: God is good, and that goodness will extend to the ways that God interacts with you.

We talk about God in terms of this deep, innate, fundamental goodness when we say things like "God is good all the time." Part of what we're saying is "I can trust that God is good when the world around me is falling apart or when everything is going my way. God is always good."

When God gives Moses an introduction to God's character, here are some of the words that are spoken: God is "abounding in goodness and truth."[4]

Look, I'm not a "proof text" kind of guy, but this is one that is just squished all through Scripture. Here's a small sampling:

- We're told we should "give thanks to the LORD, for he is good." (1 Chronicles 16:34)
- God "is good; his love toward Israel endures forever." (Ezra 3:11)
- "Good and upright is the LORD." (Psalm 25:8)
- If I live in God's house, "goodness and love will follow me all the days of my life." (Psalm 23:6)
- "The LORD is good to all; he has compassion on all he has made." (Psalm 145:9)
- "No one is good—except God alone." (Mark 10:18)
- "I remain confident of this: I will see the goodness of the LORD in the land of the living." (Psalm 27:13)
- "They celebrate your abundant goodness and joyfully sing of your righteousness." (Psalm 145:7)
- "You are good, and what you do is good; teach me your decrees." (Psalm 119:68)
- "Teach me to do Your will, For You are my God; Your Spirit is good. Lead me in the land of uprightness." (Psalm 143:10, NKJV)

There are more! Scripture often speaks of God's goodness. Sometimes that goodness is equated with God's actions (the goodness of God leads God to act). Sometimes it's just a description of God's character. We're told to be thankful for God's goodness, to praise God for it, and I particularly love Psalm 143:10, where the psalmist says, "Your Spirit is good. Lead me in the land of uprightness" (NKJV). What he's saying is the Spirit is good and can lead me to do the right things.

God has made us in the image of God, which means even in our creation we can't have been without goodness. Being made in God's image, who is good, requires that at least some of who and what we are must be good as well. And, of course, the Holy Spirit gives us a new heart, and the growing presence of the Spirit in our lives moves us toward goodness. Jesus said that the Holy Spirit would "guide [us] into all the truth."[5] And look at this amazing verse from Ezekiel, where God is telling the people of Israel how their lives will change as they come to God: "I will give you a new heart and put a new spirit in you; I will remove from you your heart of stone and give you a heart of flesh. And I will put my Spirit in you and move you to follow my decrees and be careful to keep my laws."[6]

Or think back on what God said on the sixth day of creation. Looking at humanity, God said we were "very good."[7] We were made in God's image, and God looked at us and saw that in us. Of course that was marred by the Fall, but it didn't completely remove the goodness of God from us—we are still God's image, every single one of us.

Even Paul, the guy who wrote that "no one is righteous," says in the same book that he knows the Romans are "full of goodness."[8] He tells the Thessalonians that he prays that God will fulfill their "every desire for goodness."[9] That should suggest to us that the narrative I grew up with—"You are horribly evil, and your heart can't be trusted to want the right things"—can only be part of the story. That rather, Paul and the arc of Scripture and the heart of God are bent toward the movement and transformation of the human heart toward goodness. We can only see humanity or ourselves as primarily or only evil by reading the Scripture without full context. And this is especially true once the Holy Spirit is in our lives. The seed of the Spirit grows to fruit as goodness in our lives. Not good deeds but goodness.

The Good Heart

I realized as I was working on this chapter that I was struggling to think of something practical to share about goodness. I couldn't think of any advice to give on how one becomes good or how to push toward goodness or five easy steps to utilize goodness when you're in a disagreement. I was getting focused on myself and what I could do to become good. But goodness isn't something that is accomplished by my hard work—it's the work of the Holy Spirit.

Good theology doesn't make one a good person. I can get my various theology degrees and study hard and listen to podcasts and read the Bible and have bulletproof, orthodox beliefs and still be unkind, unpleasant, even evil. We don't have to think about it long to come up with examples of people like this. And, as James said, even the demons believe that "there is one God" and tremble.[10] Good theology is not a guarantee of goodness.

The only guarantee of goodness is the goodness of God. God creates goodness in us. Which is why goodness is not about doing but about being.

As we're trying to discern and move toward a greater understanding of goodness in our conflicts and disagreements, we should probably look back at why Paul is talking about the fruit of the Spirit at all. He's talking about when Christians get in horrible fights with each other and how we can tell if we're entering those arguments empowered by the Spirit or not. Paul says that the entire law—every rule of God— can be fulfilled by following a singular rule: "Love your neighbor as yourself."[11]

So the true mark of goodness may well be the transformative power of loving one's neighbor, emerging from our lives as a deeply rooted part of our being.

In the ways and forms I love my neighbors—however a neighbor shows up in my life—I can see where goodness is growing in me and the places that have not yet been transformed. Just this afternoon, for instance, when I should have been writing this chapter, I got into a fight on social media. Now, there can be good reasons to fight on social media. There can even be loving reasons for it. But as I pushed harder into a disagreement with a single individual, I realized that my deepest motivation had become to punish him for the way he was speaking to me and others. And the best and easiest way to punish someone online is to shame them in some way.

I realized with every reply to this guy that I was wrestling more and more with the desire to just smash and really embarrass him in front of the whole virtual world. And I mean it when I say *wrestling*. There was this part of me that wanted to crush him and this other part that was working to prevent that action. I would type a response and then delete it.

He was being cruel and dehumanizing, which made my impulses feel justified. He was writing from an anonymous account, which made it harder to think of him as a person. It was difficult to see him as my neighbor, let alone love him.

What I typically want to do when telling a story like this is end it by saying "and then I destroyed him and felt bad about it," or "and then I disengaged," or "then I sent him a private message and we became friends." And at different moments in my life, I have done all those things.

But you see, none of those actions would have made me good or bad (though at least one of them could be a sin). The whole point of this chapter is that the goodness of heart that comes from the Holy Spirit . . . comes from the Holy Spirit. In this situation, it definitely was goodness holding me back from wanting to crush this guy—a situation that sounds suspiciously like what I was told as a kid: Fight against your own evil desires.

Ah, but I'm not completely good yet. And I think that the goodness was deeper in my heart than my desire to do harm. It's complicated. But I can look at my life when I am more intimate with God and see goodness increasing in me.

Am I a "good person"? Well, there's some goodness in me, and I am hopeful that the Spirit's continued presence in my life will only increase that.

So let's, like Paul, pray for each other that God will fulfill our "every desire for goodness." And as our goodness grows, we can move away from legalism, our external attempts to force goodness. Rules aren't necessary for those whose hearts draw them on toward good things. When we allow our love for others to guide us, the Holy Spirit's goodness will increasingly well up and overflow . . . even in the midst of complicated disagreements.

Kathy

There is so much here, Matt. I'm going to start with your point about legalism because that's so often what Christians do to try to manufacture goodness. But I think there's often a double standard. Men get so many excuses for their behavior—starting from childhood because "boys will be boys." We may have been taught that our desires are evil, but I have always felt that because boys/men in certain cultural circles are raised up as the leaders, they can wear and do whatever they want (since, the logic goes, even adulterous and murderous King David was a man after God's own heart).

Summer-camp packing lists often require "modest" one-piece

bathing suits for girls while boys can run around half naked. School dress codes have rules around spaghetti straps, crop tops, and the length of shorts—but only for girls. It reminds me of the evergreen conversation around why women should not be ordained for ministry, which boils down to the argument that "we are universally a stumbling block to men." Apparently some men are not handsome enough to be a distraction.

Ironically, all this emphasis on external goodness messes up our understanding of ourselves, our bodies, and one another. The emphasis on modesty and certain body types as good, attractive, and desirable negatively impacts all of us.

Our cultural obsession with the outward, purely superficial appearance of goodness shows up everywhere. I posted some professional photographs of my family on social media, using them to talk about the value of taking as many quality family photos as you can, especially as your children get older and time together is hard to find. As the comments and likes climbed, many people talked about how beautifully coordinated we looked. (I don't know if anyone noticed that two family members were wearing gym shoes.) That's often what goodness actually looks like or is emphasized as in our faith circles. It's about external behavior, when what Christians really ought to be examining are internal motivations.

I appreciate you ending with a nudge to move away from legalism to a deeper understanding of how Christians ought to consider *our* behaviors not only being labeled as "good" but also being for the common good.

Did dancing ever lead to you stumbling, Matt? In other words, how has an incorrect understanding of goodness impacted your understanding of yourself and others? How did that shift for you, and how has that shift into this more holistic understanding of goodness impacted your understanding of God and how you see others?

Matt

Great questions. Let me share two things about how it impacted me, one major thing about how it impacted my view of others, and one thing about how it impacted my view of God.

The two things about myself are this: Misunderstanding goodness made me less likely to do good for others and more likely to call things sin that are not sin. First, thinking of myself as my own worst enemy (the depraved, lawless self that wanted to destroy all) sent me into spirals of uncertainty when I set out to do something good. *What's my real motivation here? Am I trying to get people to notice me? Am I hoping some benefit will come to me?* Ironically, this certainty that I was "the worst" actually made me worse. Yes, sometimes my motives can be mixed. That doesn't mean the good deed shouldn't be done. Sometimes my motives are purely evil (it happens). And sometimes there's a good thing I want to do because it's good. Constantly searching for a sinful motive in my good behavior wasted a lot of time and skewed my self-image.

Second, the "dancing causes you to stumble" line of thinking leads to a lot of pronouncements of sin on things that are neutral or—even, sometimes—good things. Imagine that "falling" into sin is literal. There's a chasm that if you step into it, you're sinning, and you fall. So you think, *Well, I'll build a guardrail to keep myself from that.* Then maybe we put up a sign: "Don't sit on the guardrail." Then post a guard to watch the rail. Then build a gate you have to go through to get to that area. Then another sign, another rail. Maybe some electric wire. So if the "sin" is some sort of immoral sex, your guardrails might be things like "don't be alone with someone" or "don't dance" or "be careful what I wear" or "be careful what other people wear."

Which brings us to the question: Is it sinful to dance? Sinful to be alone with someone? Sinful to wear spaghetti straps? And the answer to all those things is no. (Okay, *could* they be sinful? Sure. Maybe I am dancing to seduce someone I shouldn't. Sure. Sinful. Could dancing be sinful for a specific individual because of something in their past? Yeah, could be. Is it broadly sinful? No.) But for years my misunderstandings about goodness led me to condemn behavior in myself or others that wasn't sinful at all. And in the most extreme cases, these "fences" actually prevent us from morally good things. I remember an extreme case where a man refused to be alone with his mom to "avoid the appearance of evil." Buddy, no one was thinking that!

And here's how my misunderstanding of goodness changed my interactions with others. Kathy, you and I each used to work in full-time Christian ministry. We're often told that the number-one reason missionaries leave the mission field is other missionaries. And this is true. Turns out that when missionaries get in a fight, most of them don't fast and pray until they come to unanimous harmony.[12]

In our disagreements with other believers, it's easy to get wrapped up in the narrative that they are terrible people. Sometimes I believed that. Sometimes I still wonder. But what Scripture tells us is that if the Holy Spirit is in their lives, then goodness is always growing in them. Which means that even if they are horrible on some topic, there is hope that the Holy Spirit will lead them to a place of goodness. Which means I can walk in with the assumption that there is goodness in the people I'm having conflict or disagreement with.

How has it impacted how I see God? I always thought God was good. But I guess it has made me more confident of God's loving approval to know that even before I was a Christian, I was still made in God's image—and that image is only getting stronger as the Holy Spirit grows in me.

CHAPTER 8

GREAT IS MY FAITHFULNESS BECAUSE IT'S RIGHT

When Faithful People Disagree

Kathy

SOME OF THE MOST FAITHFUL PEOPLE I know are people with whom I disagree. I met them at the marches and protests I covered as a newspaper reporter. I've engaged with them more recently through social media. I unfriended a few and a few have unfriended me during presidential election cycles and contentious political seasons. We all faithfully went to Bible studies and prayer meetings throughout high school and college. And some of us call ourselves faithful Christians.

These days, though, many of them question my faithfulness because a mature Christian ought to attend weekly church services, which I currently do not, or because I make everything about race when Jesus was colorblind (he was not) or because my political and theological leanings have shifted over time. For my part, I question what is at the root of their loyalty to institutions and tradition and what motivates them on certain political issues and how they can ignore the role race plays in our daily lives. If we're going to understand faithfulness, we probably need to find ways to talk with each other instead of at or about each other.

What Is Faithfulness?

Every morning when I swing my legs off the bed and step down, I fully believe there will be a floor to catch me. This isn't faith. I know there is a floor beneath me, whether I can see it or not. The floor exists, so it doesn't take a leap of faith for me to crawl out of bed and step down.

Depending on the theological depth of our Sunday school experience, some of us (I'm raising my hand) were told that faith is a lot like our first step in the morning or the act of sitting down in a chair. We just assume that the chair will hold us, and that assumption is "faith." But it's not.

Faithfulness is faith in action, the act of believing and trusting. One can claim to have faith, but it is the outward expression— faithfulness—that allows others to engage with your proclaimed beliefs. For Christians, our faith is in God's goodness, despite what is happening in the world around us. Faithfulness also doesn't start with me or you. It starts with God and God's faithfulness. God's faithfulness isn't about making any one individual's life perfect, nor is it about making sure everyone gets to heaven. God's faithfulness is simply who God is, and that faithfulness is expressed for the whole of creation—the earth, the animals, and the people. God created it all and looked at it all and called it all very good.

Matthew 6:25-34 is often used to teach on the futility of worry, but the reason why Christians need not worry is because God is faithful. Jesus' examples? Nature. "Look at the birds of the air; they do not sow or reap or store away in barns, and yet your heavenly Father feeds them. Are you not much more valuable than they?"[1] God faithfully provides for creation—for the birds and the lilies and the grass of the field. Imagine how that faithfulness is expressed for us as the ones created in God's own image.

What I find so challenging is that faithfulness is not only found in the people with whom I share values and beliefs. Friends and acquaintances of different faith traditions are just as, if not more, faithful to their practices and rituals. I continue to learn a lot from Muslim friends and acquaintances as they observe Ramadan; they fast, reflect, and pray for a month. The closest thing I see in my Protestant circles is Lent, when friends are giving up social media, chocolate, and alcohol. I'm a yoga teacher and practice yoga, and through those relationships I've met people who do not necessarily subscribe to a single faith tradition but practice nonviolence, becoming vegetarians because of the harm eating animals does to animals and to the earth. I've had several yoga clients whose commitment to nonviolence extended to bugs. They've scooped up ants, spiders, and stink bugs from doorways and instead of doing what I do (squish), they take them outside. Yes, it's happened during class.

Christians have not cornered the market on faithfulness. Christians are not God's only image bearers. Even in the United States, with its ongoing movement among some groups to operate as a Christian nation, non Christians are no less faithful to their beliefs.

Then why does Christian faithfulness matter? It matters because as Christians, we believe God's faithfulness and love for the world is Good News for everyone. The way Christians should live, the way we show up in our neighborhoods and not just our places of worship, should reflect that goodness for everyone, even when we disagree.

Public, Not Private

The fruit of the Spirit isn't meant to be a secret. Fruit starts with a seed. The plant or tree flowers, and those beauties invite pollinators to do their thing. The beauty of the flower, the potential fruit, draws bees to transfer the pollen, which then triggers the flower to become the fruit. Fruit is food, and food is communal. It is shared and weighs down tables with love and fills the air with the smells of steaming rice, garlic, soy sauce, and chili peppers in various forms. You'll notice at large tables in Chinese restaurants that there is a lazy Susan at the center of the table. It's a big one holding all the dishes served because the meal is meant to be communal and shared. That is how I envision the fruit of the Spirit. My faithfulness isn't meant just for me to get into heaven. It's meant to draw others into curiosity about Jesus and to be shared because it is beautiful, life-giving.

But so often how faith and spirituality are labeled and lived out in the world is strange and distorted, not beautiful. I often hear politicians and pastors speak about personal rights, free will, and how God might bless America. As of this writing, several politicians are fully owning the label of Christian Nationalist, with the tacit and even vocal approval of their churches and pastors, and Texas public schools require the story of Moses as part of its US history curriculum. All these examples presuppose that Christianity is inherently a public faith. But meanwhile, a long list of politicians and pastors, when caught breaking the law or Christian codes of conduct, appeal to the language of "private faith" to relativize the significance of their scandals. The language of spirituality is regularly used as a tool wielded for political and personal gain for a specific group of people at the expense of others. (It is important to remember here that the US is not a Christian nation. There is no national or state religion, which allows for a diversity of beliefs to coexist and thrive alongside one another.)

Certainly privacy is not on its own an invitational faith, yet our spiritual practices have private components. I think of my elders—my halmoni (grandmother), who is now with Jesus; and my parents, who still pray every morning for their children, son-in-law, seven grandchildren and their future spouses, and future great-grandchildren. The practice in the Korean immigrant church is a communal one—sunrise prayer or sae-byuk gi-doe—but if you are not connected to a Korean Christian or other church community, this type of prayer becomes private by default.

Morning quiet times are a common private spiritual practice, though they once were quite the source of guilt for me simply because I have never been a morning person. I could never have a coherent quiet time before tending to the realities of work and family life. Memorization of Bible verses is generally private, though it can become communal and even competitive. And then there's the most private of faith practices: tithing and offering. Modern technology allows us to tap into apps and let people see what we're reading in the Bible and our devotionals, but I have yet to see anyone come up with a Tithing Today app to track and share what we are giving.

And yet the fruit of the Spirit cannot be hidden in the privacy of our lives. Our faithfulness, like all aspects of the Spirit-filled life, is meant to have a noticeable impact on the lives and world around us. Faithfulness supports the Spirit's work, transforming our reactions and relationships with love and patience and kindness. Our love isn't fickle—it's faithful, even when we aren't "in love." Our patience isn't dependent on the circumstance—it's faithful, even when we are worn thin and at our limit. Our kindness doesn't play favorites—it's faithful, freely given even to the people with whom we have the deepest of disagreements. We believe in a faithful God, so we show up. Faithfully.

Make It Known

I'm just beginning to unpack the ways growing up as an immigrant and ethnic minority made it both necessary and more comfortable to have a private faith. My first language was Korean, and until I was in the later years of elementary school, Sunday school was in Korean.

Once we moved to the suburbs and Moody Bible Institute students did their internships teaching Sunday school, my faith language shifted to English. But because my family still attended a Korean-speaking church, my faith was extremely private. Unless I was willing to serve as an interpreter during the worship service or a friend was okay being the only non-Korean in Sunday school next to the intern, church was separate from my life outside of Sunday.

One of the internal bridges between the two languages of my faith is hymns. I grew up singing hymns in Korean, not only in church but also during the epic road trips to various national parks my parents planned out each summer. Slowly I would learn these classics in English as I entered more English-speaking Christian spaces.

"Great Is Thy Faithfulness," by Thomas Obadiah Chisholm, is a favorite of mine. I once knew at least the first verse by memory in Korean, sung in three-part harmony. Dad would sing tenor, and Mom, my sister, and I would try to carry the harmony and alto lines.

> *Great is thy faithfulness, O God my Father,*
> *there is no shadow of turning with thee.*
> *Thou changest not, thy compassions, they fail not;*
> *as thou hast been, thou forever wilt be.*

> *Great is thy faithfulness!*
> *Great is thy faithfulness!*
> *Morning by morning new mercies I see;*
> *all I have needed thy hand hath provided.*
> *Great is thy faithfulness, Lord, unto me.*[2]

Singing hymns in the car may have had a more profound impact on my spiritual life than the revolving door of English-speaking interns (except for John Bezel, the one Sunday school teacher who never made fun of the Korean food or smells he encountered, and who shared the gospel with me). We sang words about God and Jesus and the Holy Spirit in a language my parents dream in and I have partially lost. We sang about God's faithfulness while driving through national parks so that my parents could see more of the country they now called home. We sang "Amen" in harmony as we drove through mountains and valleys, and every Sunday my parents would find a local church—Korean-speaking or not—to be in God's presence with other believers.

My parents may have been trying to instill the value and practice of attending Sunday service, but what they did was teach me what faithfulness could and should look like. It was uncomfortable to walk into a very white congregation in Tennessee or Florida or Colorado and be greeted less with warmth and welcome and more with curiosity and suspicion. It was uncomfortable and awkward to walk into a small chapel and ask the pastor if we could have a short family service in the back pews since we had missed service. It was horrifying to teenage-me to walk into a Korean immigrant church and be surrounded by new aunties and uncles whose heart-language welcome was a relief for my parents.

But when I look back, still working through some of my emotional baggage, I see how my parents' faithfulness invited me to live an uncomfortable faith in a culture inside and outside the church that still emphasizes comfort. They crossed cultural and language barriers before it became a thing white churches talked about, and they invited our non-Korean hosts to learn to welcome the stranger on the fly. Their faithfulness always started with God's faithfulness, and then it planted seeds not only in me but also in the people we encountered during our road trips.

Back to my favorite hymn. It's important to mention that Chisholm served one year as a minister of the Methodist Episcopal Church, South. He resigned due to poor health and then worked as a life-insurance agent, writing the lyrics to "Great Is Thy Faithfulness" in 1923, inspired by Lamentations 3:22-23.[3] The Methodist Episcopal Church, South denomination was formed in 1844 by pro-slavery Methodists.[4] Imagine your life-insurance agent writing lyrics that would be sung a hundred years later and finding out that the church she attended believed it was okay to enslave people. That is the complex reality of a faith tradition that spans time. Not everyone and everything produces fruit free of blemishes.

But I also see that as an invitation to all of us to consider the ways we hesitate to live our faith loudly and fully into all the spaces we help fill. Sadly, the church doesn't have the reputation as a place where people can just be human and imperfect. It's human to hesitate when we feel judged, and that hesitation leads to missing what faithfulness means. We end up reducing faithfulness to superficial performances of obedience or belonging. We define faithfulness in ways that become a ticket into a community or leave people outside as an enemy.

Do your expressions of faithfulness mean something only to people already "inside" Christian community? More than wearing a cross or including Jesus in our social-media bios, how might what we say or do speak of God's great faithfulness to everyone around us and not just serve as a signal to other Christians? What little thing might we create that outlasts our physical lives, bearing fruit like a life-insurance agent's hymn living in the memories and life of a Korean immigrant?

Not All Fruit Is Equal

Faithfulness is not a competition. It is, however, measured by impact—individual and collective. This is where the private becomes public, and the Western model of an individual's faith is rightfully shattered to call into account the faithfulness of the whole church: the community of believers. The product of our faith should be measured in the way it brings about goodness in the world and replicates God's goodness for everyone, not just a select few.

Even fruit can be dangerous. I enjoy grapefruit and starfruit, though it's difficult to get to the edible part (no, I will not buy grapefruit spoons or pre-cut fruit). But both fruits can have dangerous interactions with certain medications. Those pretty berries on your evergreen? Well, if it's a yew, those berries are poisonous. Period.

Not every fruit produced is safe and good. It may look beautiful, and maybe the first bite or two or three are fine, but over time and in larger amounts, certain fruits are toxic for some people, and others are toxic for everyone.

A certain kind of faithfulness may look good from the outside and at first glance seem quite harmless, but faithfulness isn't rooted in single actions but in repeated behavior over time. That repeated behavior can look beautiful depending on your proximity and exposure, but the long-term trajectory and impact may produce harm instead of healing.

I've shared some of the Korean American church's beautiful legacy—a commitment to prayer and cross-cultural ministry within its own community. In the past few years, we saw the more painful parts of that legacy revealed as a significant Korean American pastor and other pastors and spiritual leaders who were shaped by this church were called into repentance. It is not a new scenario. In fact, we are seeing it happen in the Southern Baptist Convention, which is, as I write this chapter, under federal investigation for the way leaders handled reports of sexual assault. Leaders in the SBC and in a Midwest Korean American church, the ones with spiritual and institutional power, thought they were being faithful. They point to all the good that was accomplished in ministry—good they were protecting, they say, through their choices. I'm sure that there were good things accomplished and that individuals and maybe even communities experienced God's goodness. Yet we must still return to the whole of the harvest and look at the whole of the fruit. If our faithfulness is rooted in a loving God, we should not be afraid to look at the imperfections and the rot. Our God wants what is good and beautiful for all of us, not just for the lucky ones, and he wants to help us all with the imperfections and rot.

Unfortunately, what reality more often looks like is Christian leaders doubling down and asking survivors of abuse to look at the examples of good and ignore the rot and infection. They point to the number of baptisms or people who came to faith in hopes we ignore the poison still at the root.

When I think of poison at the root, I think about teeth. Maybe it's because I'm married to a dentist and have learned why putting off a root canal can lead to losing the entire tooth. When church leaders ignore the pain and look elsewhere, they are only covering up the infection that will lead to the eventual death of the root, which will require a complete extraction. If they fight the need to attack the rot, they run the risk of that rot infecting the whole tooth.

That is not faithfulness. Faithfulness doesn't produce rot. I hold tightly to that promise as I think about the ways in which my theological beliefs continue to shift. My desire to live faithfully compels me to revisit beliefs and practices. I think about the ways in which my current beliefs do not align with those of my parents, whose faithfulness set into motion my belief in Jesus. Over the past decade, my parents and I have had several disagreements about politics, how the church addresses divorce and sexuality, and what I publicly support or share on my social media. I don't need to go to social media to find conflict and disagreement.

But I pray that our faithfulness continues to invite us together, even when it's uncomfortable or awkward. Because in our commitment to faithfulness—true faithfulness, rooted not in sameness but in discernment—we will find ourselves together in God's presence in ways that live out the Good News for our extended family and communities.

Matt

I love the way Kathy talks about faithfulness as a community in this chapter. There were so many things about Kathy's family that were reflected in my own family growing up. My parents took me and my sisters on epic road trips in the summers too. And Mom always made sure that we stopped at church somewhere on Sundays, even if it wasn't always "our" kind of church. I grew up Baptist, and I vividly remember the first time I took Communion—at the front of the church, as an eight-year-old, in a Presbyterian congregation—with wine instead of grape juice. I thought something was wrong. I made a loud noise and a face and said, "Something is wrong with this grape juice!"

Or the time when we visited an African American congregation and were the only white family. Unlike Kathy's family, ours was treated with great kindness and honor when we showed up (though I am sure there must have been some trepidation about these white folks arriving unannounced). Everyone made sure to come say hello to us. Years later, when I was in college, I didn't think anything of going to Black churches by myself because when I was a kid our family had gone and had a good experience (even though we were significantly underdressed!).

Something I'm reflecting on after reading this chapter are Kathy's thoughts about how faithfulness pushes us into relationships with other faithful people, despite the fact that we disagree about important things—because we agree about Jesus, someone more important than those other disagreements.

My wife, Krista, and I are going through a churchless moment right now, too, by which I mean we don't have a regular place we worship weekly. Part of that is pandemic related—we were in the process of seeking a new regular place when the COVID-19 pandemic hit—but another part is because of basically two things: theology and comfort. Theology because over the years some theological non-negotiables have become part of our belief system, which eliminates a lot of churches from being places that I see as healthy for my wife and kids. (For instance, I don't want to take them to a church that doesn't allow women to participate as full members of the body of Christ.)

And part of it is comfort. Most of the churches where we fit theologically have a completely different culture from what I grew up with. Different music, different ways of doing Communion, different traditions. (We showed up on "Pentecost Sunday" one week and were shocked to see that everyone was wearing red, which is apparently a tradition in many churches. We had never been in a church that even celebrated Pentecost as an annual thing.) So my need to find people who agree with me in the community (or a community where theological diversity is celebrated!), and our preference to find a place that's comfortable, has led to difficulty in finding a church home.

But just yesterday, Krista told me, "I'm ready to go back to church. We need to find a place." That desire for faithful community is drawing us back. Even though we can't find a place that's comfortable. Even though we can't find a place where our theology is in complete agreement. I'm encouraged by this chapter that maybe that's a good thing.

Kathy, I was interested in the folks who feel like you talk about race too much. As a white dude, I know that's partly because people in majority culture don't have to think about race unless they want to or are forced to, whereas minority cultures and ethnicities and races are forced into it daily. This says to me that part of the issue here is a failure on the part of our majority siblings to really see and understand the experiences of our faithful minority siblings. Any thoughts about how we can enter each other's worlds better?

Kathy

We've talked about this before because we are friends, but for the sake of our readers I'll put it bluntly: I'm already in "your" world. I am multicultural and multilingual. I speak English and Korean and whiteness. My parents gave me and my sister American names, and Peter and I gave our children American names in addition to the Korean names we made sure appear on their diplomas. Assimilation is how my family and I have gained entry into whiteness, which makes things like the popularity of K-dramas and K-pop so interesting because I grew up watching bootleg copies of K-dramas before subtitles and listening to K-pop on cassette tapes from Korea.

A good place to start might be this great monologue from *She-Hulk: Attorney at Law*, where Jen, who hates the moniker "She-Hulk" because she can't exist outside of being a derivative of Hulk, talks about their differences:

> Well, here's the thing, Bruce: I'm *great* at controlling my anger. I do it all the time. When I'm catcalled in the street, when incompetent men explain my own area of expertise to me. I do it pretty much every day, because if I don't, I'll get called "emotional" or "difficult," or might just literally get murdered. So I'm an expert at controlling my anger because I do it *infinitely* more than you![5]

So take this and add the layer of race and ethnicity—that's how I feel. (As a heterosexual woman, my experience doesn't include the layer of sexual identity.) Even before I understood how assimilation impacted my own life, I was living it.

So for white people, I would begin with the invitation and imperative to listen to a variety and diversity of non-white people and not just the four to six non-white people. Reach beyond your non-white acquaintances, who may not feel comfortable or safe with you in conversations like these. Read books and articles, watch documentaries, and listen to podcasts by non-white people, including non-Christians or Christians who hold different theological beliefs. Watch movies and shows that feature a majority non-white cast and take note of what you don't understand or are not familiar with. If you're someone who doesn't enjoy foreign-language films, sit with that discomfort and watch a movie with the subtitles.

And then if you truly have non-white friends, ask them if it's okay to run through some of your interpretations of culture or experiences of discomfort and if they are willing to share some honest experiences with you that might be painful for you to hear. Remember, this is not your starting point nor should it be your only point of reference or learning. People of color are not here to be your personal tutor in all things diversity. However, white people also cannot be their own and only experts when it comes to the realities of racism. (The same applies to conversations about sexuality and disability, for example.)

Matt, you shared about being okay with discomfort as you and Krista look forward to entering back into a church community, and that's also a place for white readers to really consider. Even in the Korean immigrant church, I was not comfortable because the older I got, the wider the communication and cultural gap became. I know my white and Black friends have experienced the generational gap, but as an immigrant we add the layer of language and culture. So again for white and majority-culture readers, think about what makes you comfortable in your church and social groups. Take note of the racial, ethnic, and cultural diversity, not for a point system but to be aware of how your physical location impacts exposure and proximity to a diversity of relationships.

And back to food because that seems to be a thread throughout both of our writing. You can love another culture's food, but that doesn't mean you love the people behind the food. Yesterday I watched several white young adults walk through an aisle of H Mart, making fun of the various foods they found that were unfamiliar to them. No, I didn't verbally confront them, but I did give them an obvious look of disapproval. I don't care if you and your children love Korean BBQ if your children make fun of the restaurant owner's facial features or someone else's accent. I don't care if you or your family member served in the Korean War (yes, strangers tell me that all the time) if you also don't spend the time to understand how calling COVID-19 the "China virus" or "Kung Flu" is racist and dangerous.

Beyond that, I would encourage white readers to be prepared to fail, to hurt people, to say something ignorant or racist. You will make mistakes. I have made mistakes. We all make mistakes. It really is how we respond to correction that shows whether we live out the fruit of the Spirit. Apologize without conditions. Ask how or if you can make amends and repair the relationship—but only if you are actually willing to follow through, which is also faithfulness. You can only ask to be forgiven. You cannot demand or expect it.

Matt

I know for a fact that you're a faithful follower of Jesus, but as you say in this chapter, you don't regularly attend church and you struggle to do "quiet time." What do you look at in your own life and say, "There's evidence of the fruit of faithfulness"?

Kathy

Hopefully by the time readers are holding these words in their hands, there will have been more justice and healing around sexual abuse in the church. I bring that up in response to your question, Matt, because I know you and I are both sitting with the reality of Christian leaders hiding abuse and leaders pointing at the "good" that abusers or the institutions they worked for or in have done in the world. Selective evidence of the fruit of faithfulness is too easily used to distract from or negate actual wrongdoing by Christians, so I proceed to answer with caution.

I can only hope that there are aspects of my life that model the fruit of the Spirit, not only by joy or kindness but also by humility and honesty. In my own life, because my inner critic is so loud, I rely on the people closest to me to recognize not only the fruit but also areas of sin, brokenness, and opportunity for change and growth. I look at those relationships as evidence of the fruit of faithfulness because these people have seen me at my best and worst and still love me and are loved by me.

We also are both parents, so this one may hit some nerves, but I look at my young-adult children and see fruit not only of my faithfulness but also of God's faithfulness. Bethany, Corban, and Ethan are incredibly loving, loyal, kind, and joyful humans. They love each other. They have deep friendships that span a decade or more. They are each discovering their gifts and skills and places of influence. Their faith journeys are their own but also intimately tied to growing up in Sunday school and in a home where we sang "Happy birthday" to Jesus and also talked about making "good" social choices.

I also hope my reputation and actions inside and outside Christian circles are evidence of fruit. Having been in vocational ministry, we both know what it's like to work and live in a Christian bubble, and we both have current experience being known completely outside that bubble. Fruit of faithfulness is when I'm known as the same person in whatever circle I happen to be in at the time.

Matt

I personally have found that devotionals are a spiritual practice that doesn't work well for me, though it works for so many other people. You're someone deeply rooted in Jesus, though, in my experience. What are some of the ways that you stay connected to God?

Kathy

Growing up in the church can mean we think God is only in the church and in Christians, and maybe we add (imagine me waving my arms around) nature. But I have tried to incorporate the practice of recognizing God in all things—nature when it's pretty is a given, but God in the forest fires and hurricanes reminds me that I cannot control God or make God convenient. This isn't a universally applicable practice, of course. I'm still not sure if I'll ever connect with God through mosquitoes, flies, or field mice.

Currently there is a lot of talk around higher education and the perceived value of some areas of study over others, but I am all for connecting to God through art. We both have daughters who are dancers—yours in ballet and mine in modern. All three of my children had the privilege of elementary-school music programs. Even in out-of-tune concerts and dances I did not understand, I was invited to see God's creativity in movement, sound, and interpretation. Many moons ago, I also was the director of worship, so even though I don't currently attend church, I am still drawn to liturgy and find a great deal of joy in connecting with God through prayers that modern liturgists have written and through those that have been prayed over the centuries.

And the hardest part of staying connected to God has been staying connected to other people. The recent years in a global pandemic were especially challenging, but even before that I found the political and theological bickering that led us to write this book had impacted my relationships and energy to engage with others. But how can we be honestly connected to God if we refuse to be connected to other people? Even monks live in community, and perhaps in more intimate ways than most of us do with our family or neighbors.

CHAPTER 9

GENTLE STRENGTH

Honoring the Fragility of Those around Us

Matt

I purposely chose a tender topic to open our conversation on gentleness because those are the places we most desperately need gentleness, for ourselves and others. This isn't a chapter about abortion, but to help us talk about gentleness, I'm going to start with an example from my time as a pro-life activist. If you feel uncomfortable as you're reading, or if abortion is a particularly sensitive topic for you, please skip ahead to the "What Is Gentleness?" heading. And remember that wherever you fall on this question (and this topic is one in which Christians hold diverse and complex positions), the whole point of this chapter is to talk about gentleness. I'll try to keep bringing us back to that.

WHEN I WAS IN HIGH SCHOOL, I helped organize a pro-life rally. We got thousands of people, all on the same day, to stand on the side of the busiest streets in our town and hold up identical signs that we purchased from the organization sponsoring the event. The signs said "Abortion kills children" in blue ink on a white sign. Or you could opt for another, red on white, that said "Jesus forgives and heals." But, the organization told us, "At least half the signs *must* say 'Abortion kills children.'"

Which was perfectly fine with me. In fact, I thought the few people who chose "Jesus forgives and heals" were misunderstanding the point of the rally. The whole idea was that you could drive for miles and see this message repeated, over and over, that abortion kills children. The "Jesus forgives" folks weren't quite on board.

A few years later, in college, one of my friends confided that when she was fourteen, her parents forced her to have an abortion. In the years to come, many other women told me their stories. They were pregnant and too ashamed to tell anyone at church. They were assaulted by a family member. Their health was at risk. They looked at the amount a birth would cost and realized they would be homeless if they didn't terminate the pregnancy . . . and they couldn't find anyone to help them. One woman had just broken up with an abusive partner and realized a pregnancy was the leverage he'd need to get back into relationship with her. Another woman shared how her baby was already dead, and an abortion was necessary to prevent her from going into sepsis.

Some of these women believed their abortion had killed a child. Others didn't. Some asked me what I thought—sometimes with fear in their eyes, sometimes through tears. One woman asked me, "Did I kill my baby?" Most of them had a story where they went to a clinic somewhere and some Christians were standing outside with signs or literature or even shouting at them through a bullhorn.

What had I been trying to accomplish as a kid, holding up a sign on the side of the road that said, "Abortion kills children"? The idea was that maybe some folks would see the signs and have their minds changed. *We could save a life, and that's worth whatever other cost there might be*, we thought.

What about all the women who went by that line of signs that day and had already had abortions? Whether their mind was changed or not, what did our signs accomplish? I imagine for some it may have dredged up painful, even traumatic, memories of their past. Maybe it made some women feel guilty or experience despair. Was there a woman locked in her bedroom that night somewhere, sobbing? It seems likely.

That's terrible, and I don't believe it was anyone's primary intent. But let's use this complicated conversation to examine an aspect of the Spirit that's in short supply in the public square: gentleness.

What Is Gentleness?

We're most likely to talk about gentleness with children and our most accident-prone friends and family. In my family, we have a giant rabbit (a little more than ten pounds—he's the size of a chubby cat) named Bruce. He wanders in our back yard most of the day, eating grass and just being a rabbit. Awhile back we had a four-year-old over at our house, and she loved Bruce. She followed him all over the yard, grabbing him, dropping gravel on him, yanking his tail.

She wasn't trying to hurt him. She was just showing him attention. And the whole time, her mom was saying, "Honey, be gentle. Be gentle. Gentle hands." "No rocks, please." "You can pet the rabbit but don't snatch at his tail." "DO NOT PICK UP THE RABBIT." And so on.

Small children don't know any better. You can't just hand them a kitten and trust they won't accidentally hurt or kill it. They don't know their own strength, and they don't know how fragile a kitten is.

We used to have some cultural norms that let us know if someone was in a fragile state. For instance, it used to be common in the US for those who lost a loved one (especially a spouse) to wear black for a certain amount of time. Grieving the loss of a spouse is a horrible, painful, difficult time. Wearing all black was a way to publicly say, "I've lost someone, and I'm in pain." It gave people cues about how to act toward that person—to give them some patience, to be careful in how they spoke to them, to be aware of the pain and hurt in the person's life.

Why?

Well, then you don't have to explain in the grocery store when someone asks, "How are you?" and you burst into sobs. Maybe someone will think twice before joking, "Ugh, my spouse is the worst. I wish I didn't have to deal with them." It's a way to signal, "I am experiencing some sensitivity. Please be patient, and please be gentle."

Being gentle requires that we be aware of the fragility of the world around us. That we pay attention to those we could harm (without intending to!) because we don't know about their particular vulnerabilities or issues.

Gentleness also requires that we know ourselves well. We have to know what our own capacity is, what our strength is. *If I push hard on this, will it hurt someone? If I say things this way, will I get across my point, or will I cause harm?*

Back in the "Kindness" chapter, I mentioned an interaction with someone who was really pushing that truthfulness is more important than kindness. The same critique is often leveled at gentleness. Wouldn't we rather have a doctor who is truthful than a doctor who is kind? Wouldn't it be better to get an honest diagnosis than be treated gently?

This contrast, a common one, is interesting and completely incorrect. Because truth is not the opposite of kindness. Honesty is not the opposite of gentleness. Our hope for a good medical professional is that they're extraordinarily skilled *and* that they have good "bedside manner"—that their communication and approach make us feel safe and understood.

When I had a lump on my thyroid and a nurse came at me with a large needle, I wanted the sample taken, but I also wanted her to be gentle. When the doctor sat down with me after the test, I wanted her to be honest, but if it was bad news, I wanted it delivered in a way that was sensitive to the emotional turmoil I was in.

We can be kind *and* truthful, honest *and* gentle. This isn't an either/or. Gentleness doesn't require setting aside truth any more than truth requires setting aside gentleness.

In fact—this is so strange and surprising to reflect on—truth telling isn't listed as a fruit of the Spirit. Now, don't get me wrong—Kathy and I both enjoy a good truth telling, especially when we're the ones who get to do it. But think about what Paul is telling us here: The works of the flesh are obvious, and they include things like hatred, discord, dissension, factions. Have you ever seen someone use "just the truth" to stoke hatred or create factions? Of course you have. It's common.

Yes, the Holy Spirit will lead us into all truth. Jesus said that.[1] Yes, the prophets and definitely Paul and even—on rare occasions—Jesus spoke difficult, painful truths to people around them in ways that don't seem gentle (almost always, by the way, to religious people). Jesus is the truth.[2] God cares about the truth. All those things are correct and right, and I'm not denying that.

But Paul is telling us that when we are caught in conflict with one another, our lives are what show whether our words and actions are coming from God or from our own sinful intentions. And gentleness is one of the hallmarks of someone whose actions overflow from their relationship with God.

As we continue to grow in relationship with the Spirit, we become more gentle, not less. We learn to speak and act with gentleness. Gentleness is a sign that the Spirit is moving in us, because there are rarely—maybe never—moments when our fleshly instinct is *I'm going to really be gentle with this person. That'll get 'em!*

Gentleness in the Crowd

It's incredibly difficult to be gentle in mass communications, whether that's at a political rally, on social media, or even in a sermon. You can't know every person in the audience; you can't understand where they may be fragile, where they might break. When you're facing a crowd, it's harder to choose your words and actions with the intention of not harming.

In fact, it's really difficult when writing a book, too, because I don't know who exactly will read these words. I don't know where you're coming from, and certainly Kathy and I are hoping that the audience will be broad and diverse . . . meaning that over and over we're debating over how to approach things, how to say it, what terms to use. And, for all of us, our intentions aren't always sufficient to prevent harming someone. (I'm going to go back to the example of abortion for three paragraphs. Again, please skip those if it's a sensitive topic.)

Take my abortion rally once-upon-a-time. Statistics tell us that approximately one in four women in the US have an abortion by the time they're forty-five.[3] If 1,000 women in that demographic saw that parade of signs, as many as 250 of them may have already had an abortion. So my stated intent with the rally (to prevent women from getting abortions) may have had a different effect on those particular women.

What's more, it never occurred to me that even recruiting people to go to this rally may have called for more gentleness. Studies show that more than half of women who get abortions in the United States are Christian.[4] And at least one study, by Lifeway (a Christian organization), found that more than 70 percent of women getting an abortion expressed a Christian religious preference . . . and that 43 percent of women who got abortions were regularly attending church at the time.[5]

It never occurred to me that whenever I said something angry about abortion in church, there were a lot of women sitting in the pews nearby who had their own stories, their own hurts, their own experiences. I never thought that my words might open old wounds or become a painful memory later.

Not recognizing the wounds, hurts, and sensitivities of others makes it so hard to be gentle. If I don't know where someone is hurting, how do I keep from poking them in painful places?

When we're talking to individuals, we adjust our approach depending on the person. I can punch my bodybuilder friend in the arm as hard as I can and he'll laugh about it because it's just good-natured fun. But I wouldn't punch my wife at all, not even as a joke. I can be gentle with my muscle-bound buddy and be gentle with my wife—but in completely different ways. If the same friend lost his dad, gentleness would mean not calling and telling him I'm going on a Father-Son retreat this weekend, whereas my wife—whose father is still with us—doesn't have any sensitivity to me talking about a Father-Son retreat. In this example, my wife needs less gentleness than my buddy grieving his dad.

This same sort of thing can be true depending on a person's experiences, history, age, ethnicity, religion, family, and so on. I grew up on the West Coast, where the word *guys* is largely gender neutral (i.e., both men and women are referred to as "you guys"—largely because we don't use the word *y'all*). But I've had female friends from other parts of the US be offended at being included in a reference to *guys*. It's a term that makes no sense in their cultural context.

As we start talking about topics that are of increasing importance to us—theology, or an issue like abortion or racism, or our political views, or something really personal like questions about sexuality or the loss of a loved one—these deeper topics can be more personal and also more easily misunderstood. When we're not using the right words for the people we're talking with, the potential for misunderstanding is greater, and that means the potential for harm is greater.[6] We see this often in our everyday interactions but with even more regularity in our online conversations, where our stray posts or comments can go far beyond our intended audience.

The Meekness and Gentleness of Christ

What's most useful to me as I discern how to use gentle speech is paying attention to Christ's priorities. Jesus always spoke with the most gentleness to those who were "the least of these" in society. He was so gentle with children, with women, with foreigners and the sick. In those rare occasions he seemed to lack gentleness, he was usually confronting people with power who were harming those around them—almost always the religious elite, the wealthy, or both.

When Jesus' followers tried to get the kids to stop crowding around him, Jesus said he wanted the kids to come to him. That's gentleness.

When the religious leaders tried to trap Jesus by bringing a woman[7] who had been "caught in adultery," asking whether they should kill her like the Bible says (and thus get in trouble with the Romans) or let her go (and thus disobey Scripture), Jesus weighed his words carefully.[8] He didn't shout at the accusers, "You're sinners too!" He gently told them to go ahead with the stoning, with the caveat that the person who had no sin would get the first toss. When they left, he didn't grab the woman and chastise her for her behavior. Instead, he told her he didn't condemn her; only after that assurance did he tell her not to sin anymore.[9]

There are many, many more examples. Jesus speaking to the grieving. Jesus speaking to his mother and John from the cross. Jesus after his resurrection, telling Thomas to put his hands into the wounds in Jesus' hands and side.

I read a book review once where the reviewer said the book (a treatise on the gentleness of Christ) was "trying to tame the Lion of Judah" and seemed to have forgotten that Jesus flipped tables in the Temple. (The table-flipping example is one that gets brought up every time someone starts talking about kindness, gentleness, et cetera)

But—keeping in mind gentleness as knowing our own strength and knowing the fragility of others—let's consider how this idea of Jesus as the Lion of Judah relates to gentleness. First of all, this image isn't in opposition to gentleness. "The Lion of Judah" is a description of Jesus as one who will triumph over his enemies (incidentally, how did God say we should treat our enemies?). Jesus isn't described as a lion that's prowling around looking to eat someone (that, as you recall, would be Satan).[10] The "Lion of Judah" metaphor is designed to tell us that Christ is triumphant and strong and powerful.

None of which means he can't also be gentle. Kathy has talked some about the desire of Western theology for strong binaries, which can sometimes become "not this but that." One of the weaknesses of binary thinking is that it struggles to capture complexity or how more than one thing can be true at the same time. The strongest among us must work hardest to be gentle. Because their strength is greater, they are more likely to cause harm without intending it. Jesus knows his strength and power well, and he uses them with careful intention. Moreover, Jesus the Lion is also described often as the Lamb. He is both strength and innocence, the one who triumphs and the one who is slain.

As for the table flipping—again, remember our definition, and then let's look at the situation. In the Temple, merchants were skimming money off people who wanted to serve God. Worshipers would come, wanting to buy a bird to make an offering, for instance. And the merchants would say, "Okay, you can buy one, but first you have to get 'temple money.'" So they would "exchange" the worshiper's money, and there were fees involved in that. The merchants were putting themselves between the worshipers and God for the sake of money.

Jesus looked at this situation and saw wrongdoers (the merchants) and victims (the worshipers, especially those who were poor). He actually clears the Temple twice. Once at the beginning of his ministry when he makes a whip (uh oh, doesn't sound too gentle) and then flips some tables (violence?) and chases the merchants out of the Temple.[11] He does it again three years later.[12] And his point? This is supposed to be a place of prayer, and you're using it to rip people off.

Jesus knew his own strength. He's God. He could literally raise the dead, order armies of angels, call down fire from heaven. He could have caused the earth to open up and swallow the merchants. Instead he flipped a table and denounced what they were doing. Scripture doesn't tell us that he so much as punched someone in the nose. It doesn't even say he was angry—in the John 2 account, his followers who saw him do it were reminded of the Scripture "zeal for your house consumes me."[13] He knocked over the tables where they were stealing from the poor and then chased them out with a whip. Did he hurt anyone? No. Did he accidentally harm someone when he didn't mean to because he miscalculated his own strength? No. I don't see a good argument that the omnipotent God was anything other than gentle when he decided to move people out of the Temple using a homemade whip.

In fact, when I look at the fruit of the Spirit and how Jesus responded to the religious merchants of injustice, I see several indicators of the Spirit on display. Jesus was showing love to those who were being wronged. He was working toward shalom, the peace of "all is as it should be." Surely there must have been some patience involved. In fact, the second time Jesus didn't clear the Temple on the spur of the moment—he planned it. In Mark 11:11, Jesus "looked around at everything" at the Temple courts, but it's late, so he goes to Bethany and spends the night. The next morning, he comes back and clears the Temple.[14] So there's some self-control as he waits to clear the Temple. There's gentleness and restraint as he chases them out without harming anyone.

And after he clears the Temple, what does Jesus do? He heals the sick.[15] Children are running around in the Temple courts shouting, "Save us now!"[16] Can you imagine children joyfully running around, shouting for God to save them, if they thought Jesus was some angry, out-of-control maniac? They knew he wouldn't hurt them. He was gentle, and he had restored the Temple to its true purpose. The Temple was never there to make money. It was there to heal the people and teach them God's truth and to receive the praise of the people for God.

But what about our opponents? What about people who are actively opposing God's truth? The apostles James and John thought they knew. When a Samaritan village refused to host Jesus, the boys said, "Hey, Jesus, should we blow them up with heavenly fire?" And what did Jesus do? He rebuked them.[17] Hatred and destruction don't come from the Spirit.

In fact, Paul told us we should "correct opponents with gentleness."[18] That was instruction to a pastor! He elaborates: Christian leaders should not be quarrelsome, should be "kind to everyone," able to teach, not resentful, and able to gently instruct their opponents.[19] What would it look like if we held ourselves and our pastors and leaders to that biblical standard?

And lastly, if there is any lingering doubt that Jesus is and was gentle, Paul wrote how he appealed to the church at Corinth by the "meekness and gentleness of Christ."[20]

When I reflect on my past, I see that I have consistently miscalculated my own strength—I was stronger than I thought. And I also wasn't aware enough to see the vulnerabilities of others and what might hurt them. I wasn't gentle because I didn't know myself or others well. When we're addressing huge, personal, important topics like abortion, divorce, abuse, sexual orientation, gender identity, and politics, too often our instinct is to be less gentle. But these are precisely the topics that call for ever greater gentleness and even more kindness. As the Spirit leads us into all truth and conforms us to the image of Christ, we, too, will become meek and gentle.

Kathy

Talking about contested social issues, where they come from, and why they're contested is important because often these issues are positioned as moral imperatives for Christians—but underlying that is almost always a concern about power. As Christians called to gentleness, we should be asking ourselves what kind of power we ought to wield, individually and collectively.

For example, the churches I've attended have always had spoken and unspoken understandings about their theology of women in ministry, as well as gender and sexuality. "All are welcome" may only mean in the pews and offering plates—not in other parts of the life of the church, such as serving in leadership roles, preaching or teaching, or even receiving the church's sacraments. Because these kinds of social issues were framed as moral imperatives, our understanding and application of the gospel changed: We are not only to share about Jesus but also to make sure some of our moral beliefs are codified into law for everyone.

I've mentioned before that religious organizations are exempt from the Americans with Disabilities Act. I actually did not know any of this until the past few years when disabled friends and other allies and advocates have called me to learn about my ableism. I learned that the National Association of Evangelicals thought it was right and good to make accommodations so long as they weren't legally required, which means: We like the idea, but (a) we reject the premise that the government can dictate physical access to our places of worship and (b) we reject the premise that the government dictates our budget. And then I started to pay attention to where Christian events were being held and what sort of accommodations were being made, just like I paid attention to how many women and people of color were invited as speakers and attended various conferences.

How does this apply to gentleness? Matt deftly connects gentleness to power and invites us to look at how Jesus understood and wielded his power. How do we as Christians and as members of society wield our individual and collective power with gentleness (in combination with all the other fruit of the Spirit)?

Gentleness is often conflated with passivity, which is why I love the example Matt uses of Jesus and the adulterous woman. Jesus is not passive. His words and actions are gentle, clear, and powerful. Jesus doesn't sit there and play devil's advocate as we Christians often like to do in the name of "civil discourse." Jesus writes something on the ground with his finger—which I like to think is an example of Jesus connecting his feelings to a tactile physical experience—before shutting down the crowd. And then Jesus dares the self-righteous men to do what they want but without his blessing. He diffuses and de-escalates, and I think that's also what gentleness should do.

I wonder if the biblical Jesus is "manly" and "strong" enough for today's Western church. How have cultural stereotypes around gentleness messed up our understanding of what strength really is? Matt, you briefly touch on this, but I'd love to hear more. What do you think about Christians who say we've made Jesus "too feminine," which I think is a way of saying "weak"?

Matt

I am so thankful for the verse "Jesus wept." I don't know what people would be saying without that, because I hear Christians even now saying it's not masculine to cry. It's so difficult to talk about this because the culture you grow up in shapes what you think of as masculine or feminine—whether it's what color is most masculine, what affection should look like between people of the same gender, what sort of public emotion is acceptable, or what social roles belong to one gender or another. We'll put up with someone disagreeing with us intellectually, but often things that are cultural can't be questioned (especially if someone has never been outside their own culture).

Here are some things the culture I grew up in says about masculinity: Men must actively seek out a spouse. Once married, men must protect and provide for their family. Men should probably like a variety of interests that are labeled "manly" (sports, cars, hunting, et cetera). Men should wear unquestionably masculine clothes (which, again, is really entertaining as we look at clothes across cultures and time. If you're a man, try wearing William Shakespeare's manliest outfit to church. See how many people say, "Wow, that's a really manly outfit.").

Jesus didn't seek a spouse. He didn't marry. He didn't provide for his family or even for himself during his ministry (he lived on the donations given to him and was financially supported by women throughout his life). We have no specific mention of Jesus playing sports. No evidence that Jesus hunted or even that he ate meat beyond fish (he was a great fisherman). He never wore pants, and one color we know for sure that he wore was purple.

Unfortunately, when I see people saying Jesus has become "too effeminate," what they often mean is that Jesus doesn't match their cultural idea of manliness. Jesus was forgiving and kind. Jesus loved spending time with children. Jesus talked to and listened to women. Jesus was a healer. He cried when his friend died. He asked God to let him walk away from the cross. He looked down on Jerusalem and said that he wished his people had cuddled up against him and let him be a mother hen to them.

Look, at the end of the day, here's the thing: If my masculinity is preventing the fruit of the Spirit (love, joy, patience, kindness, gentleness, et cetera) from flowering in my life, then it's time to set my definition of masculinity aside and become someone more like Jesus.

CHAPTER 10

I CAN'T HELP IT

Thoughts on Self-Control

Kathy

WHEN I THINK OF SELF-CONTROL, I usually think about my parents' nickname for me: oolbo, Korean for crybaby. I cannot control my tears.

My mom tells the story of how eight-month-old me cried the entire flight from Seoul to Seattle. (Obviously I have no recollection of this, but I'm certain I must've stopped crying long enough to sleep, eat, and poop.) Another story is how when my younger sister was being punished for whatever she had done, standing stoically with arms raised up above her head, I was the one crying and asking for mercy. I don't think they meant to make me feel ashamed, but I did. What was wrong with me that I would cry when someone else was being punished? To this day, my parents will admonish me to stop crying, as if they are embarrassed and afraid of what my tears represent.

The reputation followed me into adulthood—but by then, I had begun to understand my tears differently. One time, at a women's leadership cohort gathering, I stopped crying only long enough to rehydrate. We were asked to share parts of our personal stories, moments in our lives that defined and impacted our leadership and understanding of who God had created us to be. I wept with each story, even when the keeper of the story did not. I wept because I could see each of the women a little more fully, more human, more whole. Their stories filled in the blanks that I might have been inclined to fill with my own biases and interpretations. Instead, they told their own stories. I was a bit self-conscious about my tears, but then our mentor, Auntie Jeanette, said that my tears gave others permission to cry and be fully human.

I've held on to that blessing for more than twenty years. It is a reminder that a self-control rooted in human dignity—our own and our neighbors'—ultimately helps us grasp most fully what God has for us and our neighbors. This kind of self-control, the kind that acknowledges our individual humanity and looks toward the communal good, is what enables us to step into healthy, productive, and loving disagreement.

Misunderstanding Self-Control

I received two messages about self-control throughout my childhood: that self-control was a means of survival—hiding the ways we were different and simultaneously trying to maintain those differences; and that self-control was at its core about avoiding sinning and going to hell.

I grew up "in the church," and though it wasn't the white evangelical church, my context was definitely adjacent to purity culture and what many would call traditional orthodoxy. Like Matt, I was taught more about what I wasn't supposed to do—don't drink, smoke, swear, gamble, disobey your parents, masturbate, have premarital sex, et cetera. To be clear, my parents and first-generation elders at church never talked about sex, let alone masturbation. We learned from English-speaking non-Korean ministry interns that sex before marriage fundamentally devalued us, which led to a further list of don'ts for us, outlining what was and wasn't okay in what we wore and how we behaved.

Even beyond that, as the child of immigrants and an Asian American in a white community, I was not allowed to do many things out of concern for safety and differing cultural norms. Only an act of God changed my parents' minds about sleepovers, trick-or-treating, and school dances. They never changed their minds about dating (which is—you don't, at least not in the American way).

When self-control is only about the "don'ts," it becomes a highly individual endeavor: what I don't do in order to be a good Christian, what I avoid in order to follow God. I may have been told (and said myself) that "they'll know we are Christians by our love,"[1] but I heard much more about what Christians didn't do and were against. The result of that focus was usually an individualized behavior.

But what if the fruit of self-control isn't about regulating our individual behaviors to be and stay saved (you know, faith by works alone) but about living in a way that is in harmony with and for the common good? What if self-control is not just about what you or I do individually for our own sakes—but about living and acting in ways that are for the good of one another?

Controlling Our Bodies

My grandmother taught me about skincare decades before Korean skincare became popular in the West. She religiously took care of her skin, always looking younger than her actual age and life filled with trauma and challenges.

I thought the lesson was that moisturizer and cleansers could keep you looking young, but my grandmother's skincare ritual was about much more than that. She was teaching me self-care, the act of honoring my body, of slowing down and smelling the fragrance of a drugstore lotion before gently massaging it onto my face and neck. Even at a young age, I learned that as we nurtured our bodies, we could be a little more healed and whole (and moisturized) when interacting with others.

Bodily self-control involves our health, which is interconnected with the health and flourishing of others. Often this has turned into a list of don'ts around things like food, weight, and appearance—cultural values around what looks healthy and ultimately beautiful and desirable.

But when we instead consider bodily self-control with the good of the community in view, we broaden our understanding of health to things like access to health care and to healthy, affordable food. Bodily self-control may prompt us to evaluate Western cultural norms on diet, portions, and even timing of meals. It may raise questions about who has access to fresh, affordable, unprocessed food instead of focusing on what a single individual is eating. Some of my vegetarian and vegan friends chose different ways of eating not because it was a way to lose weight but because they are considering the environmental impact of industrial farming and animal products.

Sadly, the church isn't immune to idolizing the appearance of health over actual health. "Biblical" diets have used Scripture to put a Western spiritual sheen over cultural priorities about bodies. And then there was a weird phase in churches where mostly white male pastors would talk about their "smokin' hot wives" (I hope to God every male pastor has repented and gotten over that phase). This objectification said a lot about what religious institutions—ostensibly preaching heavenly values—really thought about physical appearances, gender, and sexuality all in three words.

When the church prioritizes individualized bodily self-control over the communal good we're called to cultivate, we harm ourselves and our communities. During the first months of the COVID-19 pandemic, many Christians supported frontline workers, coordinating the donation and delivery of meals to hospitals and health care workers. Church leaders pivoted to virtual platforms to maintain and create community, and it was amazing to watch people rally to create new infrastructures. But as the months and years of mitigation efforts took their toll, many Christians pivoted in an incredibly painful and infuriating direction. In the name of bodily autonomy, Christians began to lead the charge locally and nationally against mask mandates and vaccination requirements. Christians, who had initially led in caring for the community, shifted to organizing against community protections for the most vulnerable populations. Even more discouraging was to see Christians weaponize the proabortion rallying cry, "My body, my choice," to fight mask mandates and vaccinations. All the hypocrisy and inconsistencies were laid bare. Regardless of where we individually stand on abortion, our communal posture should be for the care of the vulnerable.

Christians are supposed to be known by the fruit of the Spirit. We are supposed to live out, in word and deed, the Good News: the Kingdom of God on earth as it is in heaven. How can we say we care about one another and want to live in harmony on earth as we hope to in heaven if we can't be bothered to wear a mask on behalf of those who are vulnerable?

Bodily self-control also involves the expression of our sexuality. Humans are sexual beings, but layers of shame and control have shaped Christian expectations around sexuality, leading to a lack of adequate tools to develop a healthy relationship with or understanding of sexuality and sex.

Self-control in this context is too often used to exclusively mean not having sex before you are married because "premarital sex devalues the worth of the woman involved." I was told that by many spiritual leaders and may have also repeated that lie. I'm so sorry. I was so wrong.

This isn't to say that Christians have permission to do whatever they want sexually, but self-control is not *just* about the physical act of sex.

A better question to ask ourselves is this: How does our personal relationship to sex and sexuality add to the common good? I know that question sounds a little out there, but stay with me. When we believe our bodies are not a commodity for someone else's gain or pleasure but designed as good and beautiful, we can better understand and respect one another and truly relate to one another as fully human.

Considering all bodies as worthy of respect and understanding self-control as honoring one another's humanity should make it clear to us why racism is such a profound evil and antithetical to the fruit of the Spirit. Christians approved of slavery because they believed the Africans they "owned" weren't fully human and therefore couldn't control themselves. Christians sent (often by force) Indigenous children to Christian "boarding schools" to strip them of their native language and culture because their families could not be trusted. If you do not believe people of color are fully human—and that includes viewing or referring to behavior, practices, and traditions as inferior, animalistic, or below adult maturity—you will not concern yourself with how your actions will impact those people. Racism has exhibited itself in a lack of bodily self-control throughout our nation's history, as even Christians claimed ownership over the bodies of other human beings, abusing and controlling men and women made in God's image for their own ends.

Many white evangelicals will self-select out of and distance themselves from these examples of racism, but if you're a white Christian, how would you feel if you saw me bowing to my parents and my children bowing to me and my husband, which is a Korean custom to mark the New Year? Would you be uncomfortable or call my Christian faith into question if you saw that a traditional Korean first-year birthday celebration includes a fortune-telling custom of doljabi, where a child is encouraged to choose from a variety of objects on a table— each object representing something about the child's future health or occupation? Many of my cultural traditions and practices have been called into question by non-Asian Christians who only equate bowing with worship and fortune telling with the occult, but in many non-white cultures bowing to our elders is a sign of respect and love, more than a hug or words.

So how do we use bodily self-control to rebuke racism today? We honor the full humanity and story of every person in our community, acknowledging and fighting for their innate right to health, wholeness, dignity, and belonging.

Our approach to embodied self-control isn't meant to regulate someone else's behavior or force them into agreement with us. Rather, we carry and tend to our own bodies in relationship to the needs, preferences, and well-being of others. It is here, within the flourishing of the community, that we will find healthier ways through conflict.

Controlling Our Minds

In an earlier chapter, I wrote about my depression and anxiety and how psychotherapy and antidepressants are key to my mental health. So I know this from experience: Self-control over our minds and mental state may require more than prayer and happy self-talk. Those with depressive, manic, or suicidal episodes need a community and team of people to help care for their mental health.

Too often Christians feel like they must take this journey alone. Once again the invitation for us is to consider how the idea of self-control is not about an individual acting out of their personal needs but how, as the body of Christ, we are invited to care for one another's mental health as appropriate.

An important caveat: I believe pastors should stay in their lane, understand the limitations of their training and field of expertise, and learn the difference between pastoral counseling and counseling or therapy from a licensed professional. Many pastors may not even have to have a Master of Divinity, which might require some credits in pastoral counseling. Such pastors are especially unqualified to diagnose and treat mental health. Be a spiritual guide? Yes, absolutely. But this is a vital way pastors can demonstrate some self-control: Recognize the limits of your expertise and genuine desire to help. A pastor is not automatically a qualified counselor or therapist. And even licensed counselors and therapists need to work in conjunction with medical doctors when medical intervention would be helpful.

As the church and society learn more about neurodiversity, we must learn to recognize that self-control is not going to look the same for all of us. Self-control in mental health means not trying to force people into alignment with what is neurotypical but, instead, expanding what is acknowledged and welcomed. Increasingly we're seeing sensory rooms at conferences—spaces with softer lighting; different options for sitting, standing, or lying down; and headphones or noise machines to regulate auditory stimulation. Some churches have opted to include in the "main" service a time of teaching geared toward children, inviting the entire church not only to listen but also to welcome the noise, movement, and random questions that children are known for.

My Dear Readers, we can learn to listen well to those who are struggling; familiarize ourselves with community mental-health resources; honor our own boundaries so that we don't enter into codependency; recognize the signs of anxiety attacks, depression, and suicidality; and ask for guidance and help from mental-health professionals or social workers. When we model and normalize mental-health check-in language with others (and ourselves), we make it possible for others to flourish. I can't help but think of Fred Rogers encouraging children to "look for the helpers" and remind us that we can learn to become those helpers.[2]

Of course, this idea of "controlling our minds" has often taken another form for many Christians: a focus on what we shouldn't be thinking about. "Don't think about sinning" is really what it boils down to. But when we look at the Bible, we see that when it comes to our thought life, God sets the bar at a more beautiful place for us. What if controlling our minds is less about what we shouldn't think about and more about imagining and then creating systems and spaces and policies that reflect our beautiful God?

Shout out to my alma mater Northwestern University (Go 'Cats!) and the university seal, which includes in Latin the phrase "Whatsoever things are true" from Philippians 4:8 (KJV). What if self-control is, very simply, about exactly that? "Finally, brothers and sisters, whatever is true, whatever is noble, whatever is right, whatever is pure, whatever is lovely, whatever is admirable—if anything is excellent or praiseworthy—think about such things."

This is where we might want to listen to the artists and creatives in our churches. My writing process can look rather undisciplined, including taking breaks to clean my stove and dust my plants while I am thinking about the fruit of the Spirit. As an artist, I am most fully myself when I can express my experiences and dreams in words that connect with My Dear Readers. Self-control isn't about censoring myself but about expressing my full self through my words as a writer and about my actions in life that point toward God's beauty and love for us. What a breath of fresh air and hope we Christians could be, ought to be, if, even in our most tense and heated disagreements, it was clear we were seeing and honoring God's image in one another and working toward a resolution that reflects God's Good News for the world.

Controlling Our Emotions

Emotions are neither bad nor good but simply a part of being human. Repeat that after me: *Emotions are neither bad nor good.* Our actions are what we choose to do with our emotions. Why did little Esther grab the toy out of her playmate's hands? Because Esther felt desire for and maybe even some jealousy over a toy that wasn't hers. Why did I yell at the driver who cut me off even though he couldn't hear me?

Because I felt frustrated and angry that his dangerous behavior had no consequences. (And because I was right.)

Emotions are not unique to humans. Animals experience emotions as well. But unlike animals, Christians often equate self-control over our emotions and related behaviors as good. Perhaps this started with the puritanical values brought over by the colonizers, but this idea has extended far beyond the Puritans.

This idea of "control your emotions, or they will control you" is not in the Bible. But the admonition to control our emotional responses is often used in our culture, conversations, and churches to silence and shut down—you guessed it—women and people of color.

The message many of us received as children was that our emotions cannot be trusted, and that is especially true for women. Perhaps you already know this, but the word *hysteria*, from the Greek word for womb, has roots in what was once considered a female-only psychological condition.[3] If you had a uterus, the thinking went, you more likely than not had some "symptom" of hysteria—and hysterical people must be controlled.

Almost every single heated exchange I've experienced on social media has included at least one person jumping into the conversation to tell me that I am "too emotional" and therefore can't understand, can't listen, and/or can't be reasoned with. It's as if I am not fully human, as though my brain and ears shut off when I use exclamation points in my tweets or cry or raise my voice in a face-to-face exchange.

The nuances between emotion and action, between perception and motivation, and the long history of people being silenced because of their emotions—we need to take all these things into account when we consider self-control, our emotions, and our policing of others' emotions. Emotional self-control is not keeping a lid on every emotion or stuffing what we feel. It is, as with all aspects of self-control, asking ourselves, *How does this impact the community? How does this help the community become better and more whole?* And with the expression of our emotions and being on the receiving end of others' emotions, often self-control includes situations that can make others uncomfortable. Discomfort forces us outside ourselves; we encounter the emotional experience of another and see the need for change.

Years ago, during a performance review, I was given feedback that my anger made me unapproachable. Wanting help to work through my subsequent feelings of shame and failure, I asked for examples and then took those examples to a coach and a spiritual director.

My coach had me walk through some of the examples and then asked me if I had felt heard in those situations. I burst into tears. My anger was pent-up frustration from not being heard when I broached difficult conversations or held differing opinions and had to interject and interrupt to grab space in these challenging conversations. My coach, without missing a beat, said she could see how I would try the "nice" and civil way to make my point or be heard and then finally try a louder voice. As psychologist and author Dr. Jenny T. Wang writes, "Anger is the part of myself that knows my worth."[4]

And what is more threatening to the status quo than an unassuming Asian American woman asserting her self-worth instead of prioritizing someone else's idea of self-control? What would the Kingdom of God really look like here on earth if all of us not only knew our own self-worth but also valued the worth of others over controlling one another for our own gain? Tending to our emotions and to the ones of those around us can show us where justice has gone untended, where we or others are being missed or hurt, the places and spaces where accountability and raising our voices may yet lead to a healthier community.

In researching for this book, I came across this quote by Black poet, womanist, and civil-rights activist Audre Lorde:

> We have been raised to fear the yes within ourselves, our deepest cravings. For the demands of our released expectations lead us inevitably into actions which will help bring our lives into accordance with our needs, our knowledge, our desires.

And the fear of our deepest cravings keeps them suspect,
keeps us docile and loyal and obedient, and leads us to settle
for or accept many facets of our oppression as women.[5]

Lorde invites us to look straight at our desires, identify the emotion of fear and how fear can lead to a self-control rooted in doubt—of ourselves and of one another's humanity—which ultimately leads to settling for less than what God wants for us and offers us.

Sometimes the most holy thing to do is to be angry, to connect the cognitive dissonance from experiencing or seeing injustice with some sort of action or physical response. My mind always goes to the Canaanite woman in Matthew 15, who doesn't let Jesus ignore or dismiss her.[6] Her daughter is possessed, and she wants Jesus to do something. She knows Jesus can make this right. When he refuses (we don't know his reason, but we can assume there was a larger purpose for this unusual, even painful approach, as we see in everything Jesus did), she shows anger and self-control, kneeling and asking for help. Even after Jesus draws a line between Jews and Gentiles, this woman doesn't give in to the anger of disappointment or personal offense. Instead she does what Lorde writes about: She does not fear her need and desire to see her daughter healed. She does not fear confronting the tradition that compared her and her people to dogs. And Jesus acknowledges her: her anger and her desire.

Most days I want to scream in anger. Matt knows this, and maybe that's a small reason why he wanted me to write this chapter. There is so much injustice in the world, in my little world, that if I focus on my fear that evil will overcome, I might drown or try to burn it all down. But belonging to Jesus means you and I, My Dear Readers, have access to a self-control that fights for the good of all. That means our self-control isn't about holding ourselves or others back—it means we get angry at injustice. It means we act in ways that help bodies, minds, and emotions flourish. And it means we approach our disagreements with a healthier posture and desire for change.

Matt

When Kathy and I were dividing up who would write which parts of this book, the one chapter I told her was nonnegotiable was that she would have to write about self-control. I just felt like I didn't have enough clarity to speak to it. For instance, a number of people in my family history have struggled with alcoholism. My solution to this has been to just never drink alcohol. I figure I have a proclivity toward it, so I should avoid it (I can barely stop myself from drinking milkshakes!).

But I appreciate as I'm reading this chapter that Kathy has really teased out some ways of thinking about self-control that are bringing the topic to life for me and helping me see it in a new and more helpful way. I love breaking it down into body/mind/emotion. That's something I'll be thinking more about.

Kathy, one thing I wonder about: You and I are both people who tend toward anger in our responses to a variety of things. I wonder if you have specific advice about dealing with our anger. How about when the anger is justified? And what do we do with long-term but righteous anger, like when we're looking at injustice in the world?

Kathy

Anger is such a misunderstood emotion. Those familiar with the Enneagram will recognize that it's part of the gut triad: Enneagram 1s, 8s, and 9s. Personally working through what I was taught about anger and what anger actually is has helped me better understand my own anger, the reasons behind my anger, and how to deal with the anger in different ways.

Unpack the lessons you were taught about anger. Was it called bad? Dangerous? Ungodly? What did you associate anger with? How did you experience anger when it was directed at you? Is there violence and trauma you should work through and heal from?

Anger, like any emotion, isn't good or bad. It just is. It's part of being human. So moving forward, practice self-kindness and don't judge yourself for feeling angry. Instead identify what is making you feel anger and why. Know how you express anger and where in your body you experience it. Personally, I feel anger when I feel like I have failed or not done what I could do to make things right, and that anger can be directed at myself and others through impatience and sharp, hurtful words. Sometimes I cry when I'm angry because I'm holding in the words but my body is processing the emotion and needs a release valve. Awareness of my breathing and body helps me notice my anger and slow my reaction down before I say or do anything I will regret. That's self-control. My coping mechanisms with anger are very similar to what I use when I'm feeling anxious: inhaling and exhaling to a count of four; naming something I can see, taste, touch, smell, and hear, respectively; or touching each finger to my thumb.

Sometimes the anger is a temporary response and needs to wash over and leave. Sometimes, however, the anger is justified and may invite a different response specific to the circumstance. I think about a quote from one of my favorite books, *A Wrinkle in Time* by Madeleine L'Engle:

> "Stay angry, little Meg," Mrs. Whatsit whispered. "You will need all your anger now."[7]

For those unfamiliar with the book, Meg is a teenage girl struggling with loss and life, and she has been told to control her anger and behave. But as she finds herself facing danger and the possibility of more loss, she has a choice: She can do what she's been told, or she can channel that anger into action that could bring about change.

That's righteous anger, the anger that made Jesus flip tables and clear out the Temple twice. Sometimes anger can look like desperation, like the bleeding woman who takes it on herself to break the rules, go out in public, and reach for Jesus' cloak. I also wonder if Jesus writing on the dirt was a way for him to take a few breaths before saying what needed to be said for the hundredth time. In each of those situations, there is a plan, a calculation of what can or should be done—or, to put it more succinctly, self-control. How will our reaction change the situation? Will it harm anyone? Will it educate someone about the injustice? Should I write something or say something at that moment? Should I find an organization doing the work to fix the injustice that's making me angry and get involved or support it financially? Or do I just need to scream into a pillow and shake my body until I'm calmer? Thankfully, I think there is a lot of freedom in the action steps to take when you've identified injustice that makes you angry.

Matt

One other thing I'm curious to get your thoughts on, and this might seem a little outside the box: Do you have any thoughts about how our personal promises to one another play into self-control? What I mean is, for instance, you and I are both married and have made certain promises to our spouses. Or, of course, we often make promises to our kids or at work or in other relationships. Does this sort of "speech act" of making a promise about future behavior have some sort of value in self-control?

Kathy

Well, I suppose our word, our promises, are helpful only if we keep our promises or apologize, ask for forgiveness, and make amends when we break those promises. I think there is a place for that kind of "speech act" for accountability. I think about promises we make to people we are in relationship with, but I also think about the leaders we trust—pastors, teachers, bosses, and politicians. When they make public promises, I assume it's an invitation to accountability and community, and vice versa.

Our kids were not baptized, but they all were dedicated in church. They also went through confirmation, and I remember thinking about that part of the dedication and confirmation when the congregation promises to help guide and provide a spiritual home for the child. What would self-control look like on the part of a congregation to work and serve together to provide a spiritual landing space for all of us? Again, I think the value only exists if we remember what we promised and are willing to follow through on that promise.

An obvious example that comes to mind is my wedding vows. I love Peter, but I am not always sure I have been the most loving when he is "in sickness." In all fairness, he isn't the easiest patient, but that whole thing about "for better, for worse, for richer, for poorer, in sickness and in health, to love and to cherish, till death do us part" is really easy to say and a lot more challenging to live out in the privacy of your own marriage.

Marriage is the mirror to my heart. How I choose to manage my words, tone, and posture has a lot to do not only with my own intentions but also a desire (or lack of it) to repair my marriage. Arguments can be loving disagreements where we are both managing our own emotions, or they can be a selfish recounting of Peter's mistakes where I intend to shame him. So going back to your question about the value of this kind of "speech act," this act, whether in wedding vows or an agreement between friends, is a promise of future behavior and a map back to loving disagreements.

As I think about the different ways we live out self-control for the sake of others, I'm brought back to how doing all this on our own, individually, is actually a lot more challenging than having self-control in community. Communal self-control is not about accountability and having someone point out that you aren't doing it right but about having a community with you that wants to live the same way, make mistakes together, and then keep at it together instead of being at each other's throats. That kind of self-control requires a lot more than just civility.

RAISING THE BAR

Kathy

EVEN THE DISCIPLES DIDN'T LIVE THE FRUIT of the Spirit perfectly. I'm not sure they even came close.

They know things are looking bad. Jesus is talking about being crucified. A woman comes to anoint Jesus (he's not even dead yet, and she's preparing his body) and the disciples get angry because they see this as a waste of money.[1] It's not even their money, and they are mad. Jesus tells the disciples that one of them will betray him, and you can see their own insecurities oozing out as they ask Jesus to reassure them, "It's not me, right?" Jesus tells them they are all going to fail, and Peter is bold. He says everyone else may stumble, but he will never stumble. We know how that goes. Jesus asks for company while he is praying in the garden, and the disciples cannot stay awake. But then they get all up in their feelings and anger when Judas and the guards come. Violence seems like a good response.

And this is all before Jesus is even crucified, at which point his disciples scatter and go into hiding. Peter denies Jesus three times. It's the women who go to the tomb and are the first to declare that Jesus has risen from the dead, and of course the men do not believe them.

This is what Jesus' community looked like. Thank goodness they are as messy as I am and as messy as we are. Their mistakes passed down generation to generation long before we could bicker with strangers on the internet.

We used the framework of Paul and the fruit of the Spirit for this book, but the foundation for that kind of life, the most vivid example of what it looks like, is Jesus. And in the community he built wherever he went, we see versions of the same sort of problems we face today. Religious and political posturing. Issues of class, ethnicity, and gender. People in need of healing, of food, and of belonging. Some people were trying to trick Jesus and his followers, and some were genuinely curious about this carpenter. Some thought they might buy their way into heaven, and others weren't even sure if they could approach Jesus. Some followed Jesus throughout his ministry, and others had the one encounter and were forever changed.

Before Paul, Jesus lived the fruit of the Spirit in the flesh and in the midst of complicated humans and quite intimately with his disciples—writing in the dirt, talking in parables, performing miracles, and never telling people to repeat the Sinner's Prayer.

As we're talking about living out the fruit of the Spirit in how we engage our world and community and relationships of conflict, we are trying to put into words what Jesus did through his life. We are trying to remind ourselves and one another that the goal isn't to win a Facebook comment section but to be Christlike, Spirit-filled. (And let's be honest—going for the win on social media is a lot easier.)

Love, joy, peace, patience, kindness, goodness, faithfulness, gentleness, and self-control—this fruit is not meant for an individual to bear in isolation. Remember, these words were written to the churches in

Galatia going through conflict. Jewish followers of Christ and Gentile followers of Christ argued out of their own cultural and ethnic differences and traditions—and their bickering compelled Paul to point them back to Jesus. Paul could've chosen the lowest bar and told the Galatians to be civil with one another. Instead Paul remained Spirit-filled, encouraging them to become more like Jesus.

We can only hope these chapters give you some pause to reconsider how Jesus doesn't set an impossible bar for us. Sure, we are doing a pretty good job of messing up. So did the disciples. They messed up over and over. The disciples regrouped, bickered, split up, found their communities and circles of influence. But they kept at it—kept fighting for community even in disagreement—and we think that is part of Jesus' invitation to us. Come back together. Stay in it together. Bicker, split up, regroup, apologize, forgive, and make amends.

Matt

When we get this loving disagreement thing right, it's so beautiful and attractive to people even outside the Christian community. I think of that moment in Acts when it says that everyone shared with each other and every person's needs were being met because "God's grace was so powerfully at work in them all."[2]

But we do get it wrong a lot, don't we? Last night Krista and I went to an outdoor concert at a venue that had all these rules about bringing low-folding chairs so you didn't destroy sight lines to the stage. As Krista and I got settled in, we were laughing because right behind us was a group of Christians in the middle of a theological discussion. It was a secular concert, and we live in a pretty irreligious city, so we thought it was funny that we had managed to sit right in front of some fellow believers.

A few songs into the concert, some folks further up in the crowd got up to dance and cheer for the band. Our siblings in Christ behind us were a little frustrated by this and started shouting, "Hey, sit down!" And then, increasingly frustrated, one of them started shouting, cursing, and insulting the people who were standing.

I couldn't help thinking, as I was deep into writing this book with Kathy, how sad it was that some folks who love Jesus were talking about God one minute and then shouting at people who had the audacity to—I'm checking my notes here—stand up at a concert. And guess what? My first thought was to shout back at them because I'm here to *listen* to the concert and now, not only can I not see it; I can't hear it because they're shouting through the songs. So this isn't just an example of them doing poorly—my heart response was not great, either.

It's honestly enough to create a little twinge of despair. If we can't even sit through a concert and show the fruit of the Spirit, how are we going to deal with real problems that come up in our Christian community or in the world around us? We can't even consistently hit the bar of politeness—a bar that is immeasurably lower than what we're called to.

But Kathy's right to say we aren't called to something impossible because there is forgiveness. God knows (and we know) that we're going to mess up . . . and part of patience and faithfulness is sticking it out together.

At the same time, I wonder if God maybe wants us to recognize the huge distance between what we can accomplish—even when we're trying our best—and what God requires of us. But I don't think this gap is meant to create despair. It's meant to create dependence.

It is, after all, the fruit of the Spirit, not the fruit of Trying Really Hard.

On the other hand, I will say this: Kathy and I have become friends even though on the surface there could be a lot of reasons for us to never cross paths—race, ethnicity, gender, how we got citizenship, and so on. All those differences could create real challenges to relationships in some circles. Instead, even though we've never met in person, we share a lot of things with one another and our mutual friend group: how things are going with our kids, frustrations in our lives, challenges, triumphs, new insights, and on and on. I don't think that's because we just happened to be compatible friends. The Holy Spirit shaped both of us in our lives over the years to where we were able to give each other a chance—he helped us see things in ourselves and grow in our character and insights to become people who could be friends.

This is the thing I keep working to remind myself of: that on the other side of every screen is a human being made in the image of God. That the guy behind me shouting at the concert is beloved by Jesus (and should be beloved by me). That doesn't mean I have to stand by and make excuses in moments of injustice. It doesn't mean that I can't disagree (even loudly) on important issues. It just means that, at the end of the day, I have a responsibility to love those people too.

One last thought:

When my family moved into our house fifteen years ago, the backyard was just a bare patch of ground. We planted grass, fruit trees, and a garden. It took almost three years for us to get our first pear. Two years for the first apple. We got plums right away. I planted, my wife watered, but it was God who made them grow (to echo a famous Bible passage).

It takes time for fruit to appear, but if we truly have the Holy Spirit in our lives, we can trust that fruit is coming. Over and over, our lives should and will bear fruit. It's a high bar in one sense, but in another it's just what we expect a healthy tree to do.

May God bless us with more fruit as we argue and disagree and grow together in the years to come.

Acknowledgments

JR. Forasteros, who made sure Matt didn't make decisions for Kathy.

Caitlyn Carlson, for bringing this project together and for all the help along the way.

David Zimmerman, for assuring us that he knew who we were and that's who he wanted.

Elizabeth Schroll, who is such a thoughtful and careful copy editor, for making sure we said what we meant.

Charissa Sundust, for helping us think through how our words would be heard by others.

Julie Chen, for a cover that visually captures our words.

Jessica Adams, for getting the word out!

Wes Yoder, for being Matt's longtime agent and friend and for answering all of Kathy's questions about having an agent.

And as always, much love to the whole *Fascinating Podcast* crew.

Kathy

Thank you, Peter, for making sure I had a bigger computer screen and noise-canceling earbuds and encouraging me when I said I was ready to write again. Thanks to our kids, Bethany, Corban, and Elias. I love being your mom. Thanks also to my parents and sister.

To Janna, Sabrina, Zakiya, Tricia, Sandra, Vickie, Helen, and Angela. You will never know how much your texts, memes, links, book recommendations, social commentary, and provocative questions about so many things helped me through one more day.

And a deep bow of gratitude for my coauthor and friend I've never met, Matt Mikalatos. Thank you for trusting me to write this with you and for your pastoral and hilarious encouragement.

Matt

Huge thanks to my family, especially my wife, Krista, and our kids, Zoey, Allie, and Myca. And also to my parents, Krista's parents, and the extended fam!

To Chris Zaugg, who kept asking for a book along these lines.

And to the many people who have showed me over and over what it looks like to disagree with someone (me or someone else) and still love generously: Josh and Wendy Chen, Jermayne and Meredith Chapman, John and Amy Rozzelle, Rasool and Tamica Berry, Doug and Debbie Stolhand, Aaron Burns, Mark Charles, and Hugh Howey.

And especially thanks for the generosity, wisdom, insight, and kindness of my favorite friend I've never met, Kathy Khang.

Glossary

SOME OF THESE DEFINITIONS need a full chapter or a book to flesh them out with the nuance and detail that they deserve. This glossary is intended not to be comprehensive but to give you an idea of what we mean when we use these words. Having a shared understanding of a definition allows us to be on the same page about what we mean so that we don't get in needless arguments over misunderstandings. For example, if one of us says "feminism" and means "misanthropic misandry" and the other means "someone who advocates for social equality for women," we need to come to consensus if we're going to have a productive conversation (we prefer the latter definition). These terms are not included here as arguments for our own ideas or positions but simply to provide clarity on what we mean when we say them.

ABLEISM: Prejudice and discrimination against those who are disabled or perceived to be disabled. Ableism also involves the elevation of those who are "nondisabled" and seen as contributing "more" to society through their participation in capitalism because they theoretically "produce" more.

ACTIVISM: Direct (and thus "active") actions aimed at achieving or opposing a specific political or social goal.

AMERICAN EXCEPTIONALISM: The belief that the United States is inherently superior to other nations. In this phrase, "American" does not include other parts of North America or South America.

BIRTHRIGHT CITIZEN: One who gained citizenship "automatically" by virtue of their birth. (In the US this typically involves being born on US soil or being born to US citizens.) There's a long, complicated history to this concept in the United States and who it did and didn't apply to.

CHRISTIAN NATIONALISM: Christian nationalism is about a desire to place "our people" (Christians) into controlling authority—moral and political—of our nation. White Christian nationalism adds a racialized component to this idea (and many white Christian nationalists are also patriarchal white Christian nationalists, meaning they want only white, Christian men in authority over our nation). Christian nationalism is not about patriotism (though it's often disguised as such). It does not mean either "Christians who are loyal to their country" or "Christians who are patriotic." Christian nationalism is about power and who has it. We can see it more clearly, perhaps, by looking at other forms of religious nationalism. The Taliban, for instance, is a form of Muslim nationalism: The Taliban wants a specific branch of Islam to be in controlling political power.

COLONIZATION: The act of one group of people subjugating and controlling another group of people by force, politics, or economics, nearly always with the intention of exploiting the human and natural resources of that group.

ETHNICITY: A way of grouping people according to shared culture, language, origin, et cetera. This can overlap with the socially constructed category of "race" but does not have to. For instance, you may have noticed that on US government forms, "Hispanic" is an ethnic descriptor, not a racial one. The official US description for "Hispanic/ Latino" people is "a person of Cuban, Mexican, Puerto Rican, South or Central American, or other Spanish culture or origin, regardless of race."[1] There are Black Hispanics, Indigenous Latinas, and Asian Latinos (and yes, white Hispanics and Latinos as well).

EVANGELICALISM: Historian David W. Bebbington defines evangelicals by four points: biblicism (a high regard for Scripture), crucicentrism (focus on Christ's sacrifice on the Cross), conversionism (belief that "conversion" is necessary to come to Christ), and activism (belief that the Good News of Jesus should change the world around us and we should be involved in that).[2] Activism in this instance is often related to proclamation—an outward expression of this faith and the invitation for others to join. We sometimes in this book refer to evangelicalism in that sense and sometimes to the culture that has grown up around those theological points. Much of the criticism of evangelicals (including from within evangelicalism) centers on cultural norms of evangelicalism, meaning things that are not direct outgrowths of evangelicalism's definitional theology. (The tenets of evangelicalism do not require, for instance, purity culture, white supremacy, homophobia, misogyny, or legalism, all things that exist, together or separately, in parts of evangelicalism . . . but may be actively opposed elsewhere in evangelicalism.)

FEMINIST: Someone who believes in and advocates for social, political, and economic equality for women. Not all women are feminists.

FOOD INSECURITY: The lack of consistent access to the food and nutrition allowing a person to live an active and healthy life. This can but doesn't always mean a lack of food. It can also mean lack of access to healthy food because unhealthy foods (such as highly processed food) don't have the nutrition to keep a person's body healthy.

HOMOPHOBIA: Aversion to, hatred of, or discrimination against gay people.

LEGALISM: Manufactured goodness that comes from excessive emphasis on and conformity to a certain moral code (which may or may not reflect God's moral code).

LGBTQ+: The letters here stand for lesbian, gay, bisexual, transgender, and queer (or questioning), with the "plus" basically a symbol to say "we're not trying to leave people out if you use a different term or don't fit neatly in one of these categories."

MARGINALIZATION: The process of moving someone to a place of unimportance or powerlessness within a social group. Often a "marginalized person" is not allowed to participate in decisions that directly affect them. Not allowing people to vote because of the color of their skin, for instance, was marginalization: People were moved toward powerlessness (and when political parties today try to prevent people from voting, or when they try to counteract the efficacy of their votes, that's also marginalization). If only one generation of people leads a church, that marginalizes people of other ages.

#METOO / #CHURCHTOO: The #MeToo movement started as an encouragement to women, especially young women and women of color, to publicly share their experiences of sexual harassment, sexual assault, or run-ins with the culture that allows, encourages, or excuses those things. The phrase was first used by activist Tarana Burke. The #ChurchToo movement grew out of #MeToo and was a way to encourage the same type of sharing related to experiences within the church community.

MISOGYNY: Hatred of or prejudice toward women.

NATURALIZED CITIZEN: Someone who is not born a citizen of a certain nation but who legally becomes one at a later date.

OTHERING: Treating certain people as "essentially different" and thus inferior because of a difference of some type (commonly race, gender, sexual orientation, and/or cultural characteristics).

PATRIARCHY: Social organization around men as supreme authority in the family and society.

PRIVILEGE: An advantage or benefit not enjoyed by everyone. For instance, there are advantages to citizenship (voting is one example) that noncitizens do not enjoy. There are advantages that can come from one's "race" (that's all "white privilege" means—there are some advantages to being white that other racial groups are not afforded) or gender or education or marital status or social class (and so on).

PURITY CULTURE: An evangelical subculture that focuses on "purity" in the sense of "female chastity" with a heavy emphasis on subjective rules centered on cultural modesty norms.

RACE: The artificial division of people into groups based on perceived physical or genetic similarities (in US history and modern Western culture, primarily the color of one's skin—but also things like hair texture and eye shape). Race is constructed purposefully.

SECONDARY THEOLOGICAL ISSUES: These are nuances in theology and Scripture interpretation where two people can disagree and both can be Christians. There's a big difference between being wrong about the person of Jesus—for instance, saying that Jesus was not God or was not incarnated as a human, ideas that are contrary to the foundation of our faith—and being wrong about these other issues.

TOXIC POSITIVITY: Believing that people should "keep a positive attitude," no matter how difficult or horrific their situation, and judging those who don't. In certain Christian communities, this attitude is communicated through phrases such as "let go and let God."

TRIUMPHALISM: Excessive focus on the Christian community's perceived successes, past and present and (coming) victory, with the result of difficult or painful truths in the contemporary moment being ignored or denied.

WHITE SUPREMACIST: A person who believes in the inherent superiority of white people.

WHITE SUPREMACY: A system that upholds the belief that white people are inherently superior to people of color. This can be relatively subtle (for instance, a preference for hiring white people that is expressed as "just wanting the right person for the job" or unexamined ideas like "there are higher proportions of people of color in jail/in poverty because people of color are less responsible or law-abiding") or overt (neo-Nazi or alt-right folks today who will gladly tell you they are white supremacists). One need not be white to hold white supremacist views.

WHITENESS: Socially and politically constructed behavior designed to protect white supremacy and power, influence, and privilege for those who are considered white. (White people need not fully participate in whiteness, as it is an ideology. Being white and participating in whiteness are not the same thing.)

WOMANIST: A term coined by activist and author Alice Walker describing reforming and expanding feminist theory to include race, class, and gender with a focus on Black women, men, and families.[3] Feminism started as a movement rooted in middle-class white women's experience; womanism works to combat racism in feminism as well as sexism broadly, including in Black communities and other communities of color.

Notes

INTRODUCTION

1. Kathy Khang, *Raise Your Voice: Why We Stay Silent and How to Speak Up* (Downers Grove, IL: IVP Books, 2018).
2. Funny side note: Kathy and I have never met face-to-face. We've been cohosts of a podcast together for years, along with our friends JR. Forasteros and Clay Morgan, but Kathy and I have never been in the same room. Even as we're writing this book together, it's all phone calls and emails and texts. We have a lot of mutual friends, all of whom are astonished that we don't actually "know" each other, and Kathy has a running joke about exactly how tall I am.
3. Galatians 3:28.

CHAPTER 1 | WAR! WHAT IS IT GOOD FOR?

1. I'm using "secondary" here in the sense that two people can disagree on these things and both can be Christians. There's a big difference between being wrong about the person of Jesus—for instance, saying that Jesus was not God or was not incarnated as a human, ideas that are contrary to the foundation of our faith—and being wrong about these other issues.
2. I think the most useful definitions of *heresy* have to do with the dividing line between what is Christianity and what is not. Which means heresy nearly always has to do with the person and character of God. Some people define heresy much more broadly, and some use the word (I think carelessly) to mean "someone who disagrees with me about theology." I think we can be wrong about a lot of important things and still be truly following Jesus. Dismissing people we disagree with on secondary theological issues as "not Christian" creates a lot of problems.
3. Are there good reasons for church schisms? Sure. There are whole seminary classes about it. The more pressing question may be: If Jesus says the world

will know we are his followers by our love for one another, how is it that so many of our schisms seem to be driven by something else entirely?

4. Ephesians 2:19; Philippians 3:20.
5. 2 Corinthians 5:20.
6. James 1:27.
7. Galatians 5:14.
8. Galatians 5:16, NET.
9. Galatians 5:19-21.
10. Galatians 5:22-23, NLT.
11. Revelation 7:9.

CHAPTER 2 | A LOVING GOD AND LOVING PIZZA

1. These four words are also foundational to C. S. Lewis's seminal work on love, *The Four Loves*. See https://www.cslewis.com/four-types-of-love/.
2. The word *storge* doesn't appear in Scripture, but the concept is present. It's based on the word *philostorgos*; see https://www.blueletterbible.org/lexicon /g5387/niv/tr/0-1/.
3. Blue Letter Bible, "Lexicon: Strong's G5373—*philia*," accessed January 12, 2023, https://www.blueletterbible.org/lexicon/g5373/niv/tr/0-1/.
4. The word *eros* doesn't appear in Scripture, but the concept is present. For a definition of *eros*, see John Owen Colton, *A Greek Reader*, 3rd ed. (New Haven: Durrie and Peck, 1855), 410.
5. Bible Hub, "Strong's 26. *agapé*," accessed January 17, 2023, https://biblehub .com/greek/26.htm.
6. Blue Letter Bible, "Lexicon: Strong's G794—*astorgos*," accessed January 12, 2023, https://www.blueletterbible.org/lexicon/g794/niv/tr/0-1/.
7. Blue Letter Bible, "Lexicon: Strong's G5387—*philostorgos*," accessed January 12, 2023, https://www.blueletterbible.org/lexicon/g5387/niv/tr/0-1/.
8. John 21:15-17.
9. Shannon Dingle, "Resisting Ableism in the American Church," *Sojourners*, November 7, 2018, https://sojo.net/articles/resisting-ableism-american -church.
10. 1 John 4:16.
11. 1 Corinthians 13:1, MSG.
12. See, for example, NASB, NET, and NLT.
13. Mark 12:28-31.
14. Galatians 5:15.
15. Galatians 5:14.

CHAPTER 3 | JOY AND HAPPINESS

1. Rob Base and DJ E-Z Rock, "Joy and Pain," *It Takes Two* © 1988 Profile Records.

2. *Oxford English Dictionary*, s.v. "joy (*n*.)," accessed December 14, 2022, https://www.oed.com/view/Entry/101795; and s.v. "happiness (*adj.*, *n*.)," accessed December 14, 2022, https://www.oed.com/view/Entry/84074?rskey=VUUZlv&result=1#eid.
3. *Merriam-Webster*, s.v. "joy (*n*.)," accessed December 14, 2022, https://www.merriam-webster.com/dictionary/joy; and s.v. "happiness (*n*.)," accessed December 14, 2022, https://www.merriam-webster.com/dictionary/happiness.
4. For example, see 1 Kings 8:66; Psalm 5:11, 28:7; and Matthew 28:8.
5. JR Thorpe, "Why Do People Expect Women to Smile?" Bustle, July 6, 2017, https://www.bustle.com/p/why-do-people-expect-women-to-smile-67360.
6. Abigail Adams, "Father Dies Days after Wrong-Way Crash Killed His Wife and Children: He 'Has Gained His Angel Wings,'" *People*, August 4, 2022, https://people.com/human-interest/father-dies-days-after-wrong-way-crash-killed-wife-and-children/.
7. Bible Hub, "Strong's 5463. *chairō*," accessed December 14, 2022, https://biblehub.com/greek/5463.htm.
8. Philippians 4:4.
9. For example, see Sophie Sowden, Divyush Khemka, and Caroline Catmur, "Regulating Mirroring of Emotions: A Social-Specific Mechanism?" *Quarterly Journal of Experimental Psychology* 75, no. 7 (September 2021), https://journals.sagepub.com/doi/10.1177/17470218211049780.
10. John 3:16.

CHAPTER 4 | FIGHTING FOR PEACE

1. Isaiah 2:4.
2. Also, even in these examples, we can find evidence of how our disagreements fracture and harm Christian community. Early feminism and abolitionism worked together for a long time . . . until a political solution to get Black men the vote in the United States appeared. Many in the feminist movement felt this was at the expense of the cause of getting women the vote, and former alliances quickly dissolved over a disagreement of whether the Fourteenth and Fifteenth Amendments should be supported. And while some continued to work for both issues (Frederick Douglass, for instance, continued arguing for women's suffragist causes after Black men got the vote), others did not (in fact, Frances Willard made very public racist statements once she thought women voting was at risk). But the point is this: Regardless of the places where individuals missed seeing opportunities to move toward shalom, there were other places that they pushed for it!
3. See, for example, https://voices.uchicago.edu/religionculture/2017/06/14/813/; and https://www.jstor.org/stable/2954550.
4. Matthew 5:9.
5. John 13:35.
6. Matthew 22:34-40.

7. "But when I confront and call out the sin of people I disagree with, I'm showing love to them because I'm trying to get them out of their sin!" Jesus' most consistent approach toward sinful people was love and restoration. So if we're trying to be Christlike, our first posture should probably be, well, like his.
8. John 18:36.
9. We don't have a lot of space to go into the ins and outs of the birth of evangelicalism, but here's what I mean by contextualization. In the eighteenth century, a series of "spiritual awakenings" swept through Britain and the colonies (the US). These awakenings were multidenominational (though Protestant) and focused on reaching as many people in those places as possible, often through things like holding revivals and targeting (and in many cases creating!) schools and universities. "How do we make the gospel clear to as many people as possible?" is a question that leads to contextualization, and the evangelicals asking it were asking it in the context of white middle- and upper-class people of the colonies and Britain.

CHAPTER 5 | PATIENCE
1. Luke 8:45.

CHAPTER 6 | KIND OF A BIG DEAL
1. Quoting, of course, Iñigo Montoya (played by Mandy Patinkin) in *The Princess Bride*, directed by Rob Reiner (Los Angeles: Twentieth Century Fox, 1987).
2. See Strong's Concordance G5543 and the Thayer's Greek Lexicon entry on Strong's 5543 at https://www.blueletterbible.org/lexicon/g5543/niv/tr/0-1/.
3. Aristotle's *Rhetoric*, Book II, Chapter 7.
4. See here, for instance: https://www.etymonline.com/word/kindness. Or if you really want to go deep, it's the *Oxford English Dictionary* for you (easy link here: https://www.oed.com/viewdictionaryentry/Entry/103445); scroll down to definition II:b (or not II:b! That is the question). "Noble in manners or conduct" and even an early Merlin and King Arthur reference!
5. Blue Letter Bible, "Lexicon: Strong's G5547—*christos*," accessed January 11, 2023, https://www.blueletterbible.org/lexicon/g5547/niv/tr/0-1/.
6. My lovely editor, Caitlyn, asked if this was really a pun and she has a point: It wasn't done for humor (although I'm still laughing) or with intention, and puns usually are. So I called my daughter Zoey, who's a linguistics major. She said it's definitely a homophone, but she would just call it a typo (*but it was handwritten, not typed!*). I thought about it for a while, and then I told her that the other day I was at the bank and the guy in front of me had brought like twenty dollars in pennies. He was making the teller look at every single one and asking, "Is this one a rare coin? How about this one?" The line kept growing and the teller was getting more and more agitated and she finally shouted, "IT'S ALL COMMON CENTS!" Anyway, if you were worried that we didn't actually have a pun, now we do!
7. Luke 6:35.

8. Check out, for instance, Matthew 11:30 ("For my yoke is easy [*chrēstos*] and my burden is light"); Luke 5:39 ("No one after drinking old wine wants the new, for they say, 'The old is better [*chrēstos*]'"); and 1 Corinthians 15:33 ("Do not be misled: 'Bad company corrupts good [*chrēstos*] character'").

9. Mordecai Paldiel, *The Righteous Among the Nations: Rescuers of Jews During the Holocaust* (New York: HarperCollins, 2007), 449.

10. Cited in Kane Farabaugh, "Japanese Diplomat's Act of Mercy Is Enduring Legacy for Holocaust Descendants," Voice of America, May 21, 2016, https://www.voanews.com/a/japanese-diplomats-act-of-mercy-enduring-legacy-for-holocaust-descendants/3340070.html.

CHAPTER 7 | GOODNESS

1. *Heart is deceitful*: Jeremiah 17:9; *only evil continually*: Genesis 6:5, KJV; *born . . . in sin*: Psalm 51:5, CEB.

2. Romans 3:10.

3. *World's Finest* #222, true believers, in a senses-shattering issue called . . . "Evil in Paradise"!

4. Exodus 34:6, NKJV.

5. John 16:13.

6. Ezekiel 36:26-27.

7. Genesis 1:31.

8. Romans 15:14.

9. 2 Thessalonians 1:11.

10. James 2:19.

11. Galatians 5:14.

12. I actually thought this would be the case when I first became a missionary in my twenties. Boy, was I in for a surprise!

CHAPTER 8 | GREAT IS MY FAITHFULNESS BECAUSE IT'S RIGHT

1. Matthew 6:26.

2. Thomas O. Chisholm, "Great Is Thy Faithfulness," 1923. Public domain.

3. Thomas O. Chisholm, "Great Is Thy Faithfulness," Hymnary.org, accessed January 11, 2023, https://hymnary.org/text/great_is_thy_faithfulness_o_god_my_fathe.

4. "Abolition and the Splintering of the Church," PBS, accessed January 11, 2023, https://www.pbs.org/thisfarbyfaith/journey_2/p_5.html.

5. *She-Hulk: Attorney at Law*, season 1, episode 1, "A Normal Amount of Rage," aired August 18, 2022, on Disney+.

CHAPTER 9 | GENTLE STRENGTH

1. John 16:13.

2. John 14:6.

3. "Abortion Is a Common Experience for U.S. Women, Despite Dramatic Declines in Rates," Guttmacher Institute, October 19, 2017, https://www.guttmacher.or g/news-release/2017/abortion-common-experience-us-women-despite-dramatic -declines-rates.

4. "More than half" is actually a conservative report from studies. Rachel K. Jones, "People of All Religions Use Birth Control and Have Abortions," Guttmacher Institute, October 19, 2020, https://www.guttmacher.org /article/2020/10/people-all-religions-use-birth-control-and-have-abortions.

5. Lisa Cannon Green, "Women Distrust Church on Abortion," Lifeway, November 23, 2015, https://research.lifeway.com/2015/11/23/women -distrust-church-on-abortion/.

6. What is the "right" word? What if we disagree on which words to use? The point here is that when we're in conversation, we need to find clarity on what the words we're using mean to the other person we're in conversation with. Lack of clarity can cause unintentional hurt or harm, and refusing to find common terminology can do the same.

7. And not the man somehow? Hmm. Was he just a faster runner? How did they catch her and not him? I wonder.

8. John 8:3.

9. John 8:11, ISV.

10. 1 Peter 5:8.

11. John 2:13-25.

12. Matthew 21:12-13 and Mark 11:11-17.

13. Psalm 69:9.

14. Mark 11:15.

15. Matthew 21:14-15.

16. Author's paraphrase.

17. Luke 9:51-56, author's paraphrase.

18. 2 Timothy 2:25, CEB.

19. 2 Timothy 2:24

20. 2 Corinthians 10:1, KJV.

CHAPTER 10 | I CAN'T HELP IT

1. Peter Scholtes, "They'll Know We Are Christians," Hymnary.org, accessed April 5, 2023, https://hymnary.org/text/we_are_one_in_the_spirit.

2. See this excerpt from an interview where Rogers explains his "Look for the helpers" advice: https://www.youtube.com/watch?v=-LGHtc_D328.

3. See, for example, https://www.etymonline.com/word/hysteria.

4. Jenny T. Wang, *Permission to Come Home: Reclaiming Mental Health as Asian Americans* (New York: Balance, 2022), 66.

5. Audre Lorde, "Uses of the Erotic: The Erotic as Power," in *Sexuality and the Sacred: Sources for Theological Reflection*, 2nd ed., ed. Marvin M. Ellison and Kelly Brown Douglas (Louisville, KY: Westminster John Knox Press, 2010), 76.

6. Matthew 15:21-28.
7. Madeleine L'Engle, *A Wrinkle in Time* (New York: Square Fish, 2007), 110.

EPILOGUE | RAISING THE BAR
1. Matthew 26:8-9.
2. Acts 4:32-34.

GLOSSARY
1. United States Census Bureau, "About the Hispanic Population and Its Origin," revised April 15, 2022, https://www.census.gov/topics/population/hispanic -origin/about.html.
2. David W. Bebbington, *Evangelicalism in Modern Britain: A History from the 1730s to the 1980s* (London: Unwin Hyman, 1988).
3. Alice Walker famously explored this concept in her book *In Search of Our Mothers' Gardens: Womanist Prose* (San Diego: Harcourt Brace Jovanovich, 1983).

NavPress is the book-publishing arm of The Navigators.

Since 1933, The Navigators has helped people around the world bring hope and purpose to others in college campuses, local churches, workplaces, neighborhoods, and hard-to-reach places all over the world, face-to-face and person-by-person in an approach we call Life-to-Life® discipleship. We have committed together to know Christ, make Him known, and help others do the same.®

Would you like to join this adventure of discipleship and disciplemaking?

- Take a Digital Discipleship Journey at **navigators.org/disciplemaking**.
- Get more discipleship and disciplemaking content at **thedisciplemaker.org**.
- Find your next book, Bible, or discipleship resource at **navpress.com**.